Welcome to

This edition has been researched and written
by
Jill Taylor

Thank you for helping Great Ormond Street Hospital Children's Charity.
Great Ormond Street was opened on 14th February 1852 with only 10 beds. This was at a time when a third of all children born in the UK did not reach adulthood. Today the hospital treats over 100,000 young patients every year, many with life threatening diseases or conditions. Through the sales of these guides we will have raised £23,500 since 1998, which has contributed to the funding of a mobile X-ray unit, syringe pumps and infusion pumps. This year money raised by Cube will go towards a hoist which will be used for assisting the movement of immobile patients. We are proud to announce that a 6p contribution to the above charity will be made for each 'Let's Go with the Children' book sold this season. Thank you for your support. Registered charity No. 235825 ©1989 GOSHCC

Published by **Cube Publications**, 290 Lymington Road,
Highcliffe, Christchurch, Dorset BH23 5ET
Telephone: 01425 279001 Fax: 01425 279002
www.cubepublications.co.uk
Email: enquiries@cubepublications.co.uk
1st edition
ISBN 1 903594 20 0

Contents

Key

Price codes are given as a maximum entry cost for a family of four:
A: £10   **B**: £20   **C**: £30   **D**: £40   **E**: £50   **F**: FREE   **G**: Over £50

Schools	School party facilities, visits by arrangement
Birthdays	Birthday parties are organised here
Winter	Open all year, Summer and Winter (times may vary)
NT	National Trust property
EH	English Heritage property

Opening Times

LAST ADMISSIONS
Many last admission times are an hour before the quoted closing time.
If in any doubt, phone and ask if you know you will be arriving late.
Don't get caught out and be disappointed!

WINTER AND CHRISTMAS OPENING
Many attractions close earlier in Winter and most are closed over Christmas and New Year. If you want to visit in this period, call in advance to check!
At the time of going to print not all opening times were decided.
We have suggested you phone for opening times if this was the case!

The 'Bristol & Bath Area' is defined to group the following unitary authorities: South Gloucestershire Council, Bristol City Council, North Somerset Council & Bath & NE Somerset Council (also known as BANES)

How to use this guide

This whole guide is colour coded. The counties are divided into pastel-coloured areas as shown on the map above. The towns and attractions in each county area will be shown, within the chapters, in the same colour, so that you can easily see what there is to do in each area.

Town names within the county areas are arranged in alphabetical order with the attractions in each town listed thereafter in alphabetical order. To find a particular attraction, use the index at the end of the guide.

Whether you live locally or are just visiting, you will find an amazing wealth of diverse interests, entertainments and activities in this area for children of all ages. There are ideas for real treats and a special chapter on what you can do for free. We have highlighted price bands, places that cater for birthday parties, facilities for school trips and places that are open all year.

We hope you will discover more about the area than you thought you already knew. Please write to us with any constructive comments on the guide. We shall be delighted to hear from you. Our address is on page one.

Telephone Numbers

Should you require special facilities for someone with a disability, please call before your visit to check suitability.

Telephone numbers are provided for most entries.

Please note that there are a variety of different charges associated with different telephone numbers. Special rate numbers prefixed with:

07 ......are for mobile phones, pagers and personal numbers and costs vary.
0800..are free of charge
0845..are charged up to Lo-call rate
0870..are charged up to National call rate.
09 ......numbers are various premium rates. Please check with BT so that you understand the cost before using.

Use this guide with a good geographical map to help find your way!
Discover somewhere new, plan your route and let the children help
with the navigating!

Bowood House & Gardens p31 & p38

Avon Valley Railway p42

41708

Birdland p37

Cotswold Water Park p10

Mohair Countryside Centre p38

The Jolly Roger p19

4

Free Places

Where can we go and what can we do for free?

We all ask this question sometimes. It makes us think, use our imaginations and at the same time we can save up for a real treat; perhaps to visit one of the super places described in the other chapters! Successful days out do not always have to cost a lot once you have an idea of what you can do, and a little thoughtful planning can go a long way in ensuring success.

Within this chapter are general ideas for going out and finding free fun together with details on free places of interest in YOUR area.

How free is free?

On the following pages are details of specific places in your area that are free. However, in some cases there may be nominal car parking charges and there may be activities described within various Parks for which charges are made. Some attractions managed by trusts or charities may appreciate a small, voluntary donation towards their upkeep.

Go somewhere, do something

There are many buildings and sites you can visit that have free entry. You will find museums, art galleries and perhaps some castle ruins listed in this chapter. They all have something of interest. Tell the children about what they might see in a museum or castle and they will find the visit more interesting.

Visit some unusual churches too. It is well worth going to a county cathedral for the special atmosphere and experience. Visit your local railway station, airfield or a seaside port. You will certainly have at least some of these in your area and children will enjoy spotting trains, planes and boats.

Children can be very useful visiting 'Pick your Own' Farms and most enjoy themselves. Also many farms now offer playgrounds and animals to interest children as well.

There are Local Authority Activities from story time for the under 5s in the local library, to special event competitions. Contact the Leisure Services Department at your local Council.

Check the 'Directory of Activities and Information' chapter also for details of sporting activities. Some are free.

All children love the beach whatever the weather! If it is too dull for swimming and sand sculpture, try crabbing, beach combing and fossil hunting.

Relax and play in the parks and open spaces. Many have playgrounds, paddling pools, fitness trails or some other council provided means of free entertainment that children, especially the younger ones will enjoy. A few ideas to take with you to the Park to make the visit just a little bit different. Play games – such as catch, cricket or rounders, have races, fly kites, take a picnic, feed the ducks. Many Rangers in Country Parks organise super guided walks, some specially geared for children. Try one! Some of the best parks in the area are listed in this chapter but there are others to explore.

Go Walking

Walking is as relaxing or as energetic as you feel like. The whole family can take part and the choice of places to go is infinite. Children can burn off all their surplus energy while you pace yourself to enjoy the fresh, free countryside.

Public footpaths, bridleways, tracks and trails are spider webbed all over the countryside. Some are waymarked trails, often describing a circular route, found particularly in the forests and country parks. A detailed map is an invaluable asset when planning a new walk. Children will enjoy looking out for streams marked and interpreting contour lines. Wherever you go walking please follow the country code. It is designed to make us all recognise our responsibilities in preserving the countryside.

A few ideas in planning a walk.

A walk can include many activities full of adventure and interest to capture a child's imagination, for fun, for learning or for starting a new hobby. Below are a few ideas for adding interest to any walk.

Collecting

Collect items while out for a walk. It may be autumn leaves, stones, fossils or shells from the beach. (Not wild flowers please!). It is worth going out equipped with a bag to put things in. Young school children will love to take them home, identify them, make labels and display their own finds on a nature table. They will also delight in making pictures with leaves or shells.

Spotting

Such things as wild flowers, butterflies, animal tracks and animal dens. Children might find a Spotter's guide and notepad useful to record their finds. What a sense of achievement to find a purple spotted orchid or a fox hole with fresh tracks around. BIRD WATCHING might become a hobby after a few interesting walks spotting wildlife.

Tracking

If you are in a group why not add some adventure to the walk. Half of the group go ahead to lay a trail using fallen twigs, sticks and stones to mark the route. After a pre-arranged time, the other half of the group must follow the trail to find the leaders. Children from the age of five will love to do this, supervised of course, but older children will need no assistance. Always remember to have a place to rendezvous after an agreed time in case the following group lose the trail!

Picnics

It may be a nuisance to carry the hamper, but when you arrive at that lovely spot by the river where the children can paddle or fish with their nets, or you can all play French cricket …. Perhaps it wasn't so bad after all! Please take all litter home and be especially careful to find all those dangerous ring pulls. For the less adventurous, walks can be directed to one of the many established picnic sites.

Pub Walks

If you are planning a walk over lunch time, plan the route to take you past a good pub. Choose a pub that has facilities for children. They will enjoy a swing or a slide as well as the bag of crisps.

Town Walks

Older children might find a guided walk of a city of great interest, especially if they are interested in the history of the place. Many walks are organised by experienced and knowledgeable guides.

Water Walks

Almost all children like to walk near water; the seashore, a lake, a pond, a river or a stream and there aren't many who won't at least try to get their feet wet! Be prepared and everyone will enjoy themselves.

Route Walks

The Macmillan Way. This coast-to-coast path takes in beautiful countryside passing through the Cotswolds and Somerset. It also offers opportunities for fund-raising to help this well-known cancer-care charity. 01789 740852.

The Kennet and Avon Canal runs from Bristol to Reading via Bath, Bradford-on-Avon and Devizes. Contact British Waterways on 01380 722859. There are boat trips, towpaths for walking and cycling (permit needed if using own bike) and opportunities for hiring boats or canoes.

Long-distance paths provide opportunities for shorter walks and rides as well. Contact the Countryside Agency on 0870 1206466 for details of the three National Trails in the area - the Cotswold Way (beware steep ascents!), Thames Path and Ridgeway. Local Information Centres can give details of other paths in the area including the Severn, Gloucestershire and Macmillan Ways.

Wildlife Trusts manage nature reserves (ideal for outings or picnics) and organise family events. Contact Avon Wildlife Trust www.avonwildlifetrust.org.uk 0117 9177270, Gloucestershire Wildlife Trust www.gloucestershirewildlifetrust.org.uk 01452 383333 or Wiltshire Wildlife Trust www.wiltshirewildlife.org 01380 725670.

BRISTOL & BATH AREA

Aust, Aust Wharf, Old Passage Road, off the A403. Excellent views of both Severn crossings from this quiet stretch of road leading to the old car ferry site and from the Severn Way long distance path running alongside.

Bath, Alice Park, at the junction of A46 and London Road. This park has a well-equipped, huge circular sandpit in the fenced play area, tennis courts and a cycle track for under 7s.
Royal Victoria Park. The largest park in Bath. The huge, fenced play area (busy at peak times) contains an excellent variety of play and climbing equipment for a wide age range. There is also a skatepark, lake with waterfowl, putting, approach golf course and tennis courts.
Victoria Art Gallery, Bridge Street, www.victoriagal.org.uk 01225 477233, houses a collection of art from European Old Masters to contemporary prints. Also, sculpture, ceramics and glass. Children's workshops. Open Tues-Fri, 10am-5.30pm, Sat, 10am-5pm, Sun, 2-5pm, and Bank Hol Mons. Schools Winter.

Bishop Sutton, Chew Valley Lake, www.bristolwater.co.uk/leisure 0117 9536470. A good choice for a day out with picnic areas, glorious views across the lake, two nature trails (one suitable for buggies), information centre, tea-shop and restaurant.

Blagdon, Blagdon Visitor Centre, www.bristolwater.co.uk/leisure 0117 9536470. Interactive displays and videos show how Bristol Water ensure our water supply. See the beam engine in action, feed the trout and follow a nature trail. Open Summer, Suns, 2-5pm.

Bristol, Ashton Court, near Clifton Suspension Bridge, 0117 9639174. This Estate provides 850 acres of parks and woodland with something for everyone. Nature trails, deer, pitch and putt, miniature railway (Apr-Sept) and visitor centre. Various events in the Summer.
Blaise Castle Estate, Henbury, 0117 9505899. The Estate comprises 400 acres of wood and parkland with paths and trails. Very popular, up-to-date and well-equipped play areas cater for children of all ages. Special Events are held here.
Blaise Castle House Museum, Henbury, www.bristol-city.gov.uk/museums 0117 9039818. Set in the breathtaking parkland of Blaise Castle Estate, the 18th century building contains everyday objects from times past, including model trains, exquisite costumes and pots and pans. Open Apr-Oct, Sat-Wed, 10am-5pm. Schools.
Brandon Hill, off Jacob's Wells Road, is topped by the Cabot Tower from which there is a panoramic view of the city. There is a nature park with information boards, a variety of habitats and a children's playground.
Bristol and Bath Railway Path, 0117 9224325(Avon Valley Partnership). Equally suited to

cyclists and pedestrians, this 13 mile path is car free and level. There are access points along the route and attractions, including Bitton Railway station.

Bristol Blue Glass, relocating 2003, www.bristol-glass.co.uk 0117 9298900. Watch free glass-blowing and at special open days blow a glass bubble yourself! Open Mon-Sat, 9am-5pm, Sun, 11am-5pm. Schools **Winter.**

Castle Park, is set around the remains of a medieval castle, close to the city centre. Children can explore the fenced 'castle' playground: find wooden animals, people and 'buildings' to climb.

City Museum and Art Gallery, Queens Road, www.bristol-city.gov.uk/museums 0117 9223571. Find everything from sea-dragons, the original Bristol Boxkite and Egyptian tombs to mammals, shells of the south-west and art in this friendly museum. Special Events throughout the year. Open daily, 10am-5pm. Schools **Winter.**

CREATE Centre, Smeaton Road, www.createcentre.co.uk 0117 9250505. A thought provoking recycling exhibition and an Ecohome to interest older children. Schools programme. Open Mon-Fri, Centre: 8.30am-5pm (4.30pm Fri), Ecohome: 12noon-3pm. Schools **Winter.**

The Downs, Clifton, are a huge expanse of open space for walking, ball games and kite flying. There is a small play area near the Suspension Bridge.

Georgian House, 7 Great George Street, www.bristol-city.gov.uk/museums 0117 9211362. This Sugar Merchant's town house shows what life was like in Bristol 'upstairs and downstairs'. Don't miss the unusual cold water plunge bath and Sedan chair. Open Apr-Oct, Sat-Wed, 10am-5pm. Schools.

Hengrove Play Park, off Hengrove Way. Choose between the 11m high play dome with suspended pathways, state-of-the-art wheels park, sand and water play areas and a large grassed space for ball games. Open Mon-Fri, 11am-7pm, Sat-Sun, 11am-6pm; closes at dusk in Winter.

Industrial Museum, Princes Wharf, Wapping Road, www.bristol-city.gov.uk/museums 0117 9251470. Learn about Bristol's transport, printing and packaging industries and the transatlantic slave trade. Find a full-size mock-up of Concorde's flight deck. The harbour steam railway and steam tug operate on certain dates from Mar-Oct. Open Apr-Oct, Sat-Wed, 10am-5pm; Nov-Mar, Sat-Sun. Schools **Winter.**

Lawrence Weston Community Farm, Saltmarsh Drive, 0117 9381128, is home to pygmy goats, turkeys, rabbits, quail, chinchillas and smaller farm animals. Picnic area. Open Tues-Sun, 8.30am-5.30pm (4.30pm in Winter). Schools Birthdays **Winter.**

Leigh Woods, Abbot's Leigh, car park off A369, 0117 9731645. There are trails, a cycle track and spectacular views of the Avon Gorge in these woods which incorporate a nature reserve and an ancient British Hill Fort. Events programme.

Oldbury Court Estate (Vassals Park), off Fishponds Road. With the Frome Valley Walkway passing through it, this extensive park is ideal for walks and picnics. Large, very well-equipped, fenced children's play area.

Open Spaces@Bristol, Anchor Road, Harbourside, www.at-bristol.org.uk 0845 3451235. A series of public squares and open spaces displaying public art - striking water and light features, sculptures and landscaping. Look out for the giant beetle!

Red Lodge, Park Row, www.bristol-city.gov.uk/museums 0117 9211360. See the inside of an Elizabethan house. Open Apr-Oct, Sat-Wed, 10am-5pm. Schools.

St George Park, off A420, Church Road. An extensive park with a large area devoted to roller skating, skateboarding and BMX bikes. There are also tennis courts, a lake with ducks and play area.

St Werburghs City Farm, Watercress Road, 0117 9428241. This small city farm is tucked away only a 30 minute walk from the city centre. See farm animals, poultry, rabbits and guinea pigs. Rustic adventure playground. Open daily, 9am-5pm (closes earlier in Winter). Schools **Winter.**

Windmill Hill City Farm, Bedminster, www.windmillhillcityfarm.org.uk 0117 9633252. Visit a working farm with nature conservation area, adventure playground and indoor soft play area(charge made). Special activity days. Open Tues-Sun, 9am-5pm (or dusk if earlier). Schools Birthdays **Winter.**

Clevedon, Salt House Fields, off Church Road. Close to the seafront with lots to do in Summer: crazy golf, putting, tennis, two small fenced play areas and, at the height of the season only, a miniature railway, bouncy castle and donkeys.

Keynsham (near), Willsbridge Mill Countryside and Education Centre, off A431, www.avonwildlifetrust.org.uk 0117 9326885. Get ideas for attracting wildlife to your own garden, explore a variety of habitats and take brass rubbings from the plaques on the Heritage Sculpture Trail (bring crayons). Discovery days. Schools **Winter.**

Lulsgate, Bristol International Airport, on A38, 0870 1212747. From the cafe you can watch planes landing and taking off.

Town Parks have lots to offer families.
Get a list from the Leisure Department of your local council.

Oldbury-on-Severn, Oldbury Power Station, www.bnfl.co.uk 01454 419899. A multi-media experience at the Visitor Centre introduces the world of nuclear power. Children's play area, nature trails and picnic area. Open Summer, daily, 10am-4pm and at other times for pre-booked groups. Schools.

Portishead, Lake Grounds. On the seafront, with a fenced children's playground, a boating lake, tennis courts and pitch and putt in Summer.

Thornbury, Mundy Playing Fields. Large open area with playground, football pitches, tennis courts and children's paddling pool..
Thornbury & District Museum, Chapel Street, www.thornburymuseum.org.uk 01454 857774. A social history collection of objects and archives tells the story of Thornbury and the Lower Severn Vale. Open Tues-Fri, 1-4pm, Sat, 10am-4pm. Closed Bank Hols & for 4 weeks at Christmas. Schools **Winter.**

Tortworth, Tortworth Visitor Centre, Leyhill, 01454 261792. See rare breeds at the Mini Farm and cockatiels (weather permitting in Winter). Arboretum and shop. Children must be accompanied by an adult at all times. Open daily, 9am-4.30pm. **Winter**

Weston-super-Mare, Ashcombe Park, one mile from the town centre between Upper Bristol Road and Milton Road. There is a children's play area and tennis courts.
The Beach. Winner of a Seaside Award in 2002, it's a traditional Summer day out at the seaside - donkey rides, amusements, candy floss and good sand for castles. The beach can become muddy at low tide but there are numerous family attractions along the seafront.
Grand Pier, 01934 620238. An award winning, traditional pier with covered, pay as you go, amusement park. Suitable for all ages. Open Mar-Nov, Mon-Fri, 10am-6pm; Sat, Sun & Bank Hol Mons, 10am-7pm; Summer school hols, 10am-10.15pm.
Weston Woods, are 360 acres of woodland on Worlebury Hill overlooking Weston. Numerous paths, trails and an ancient British Hill Fort.

GLOUCESTERSHIRE

Cheltenham, Cheltenham Art Gallery and Museum, Clarence Street, www.cheltenham.artgallery.museum 01242 237431. Well-planned displays cover local history. Look out for the gallery devoted to Edward Wilson who died with Captain Scott. Trails for children. Open Mon-Sat, 10am-5.20pm, Sun, 2-4.20pm. Closed Easter Sun & Bank Hols. Schools **Winter.**
Hall of Fame, Cheltenham Racecourse, www.cheltenham.co.uk 01242 513014, displays the story of steeplechasing and its immortals. Try the mechanical racehorse! Open Mon-Fri, 9am-5pm. Schools **Winter.**

Pittville Park. A large attractive park with some of the finest aspects of Regency Cheltenham, ornamental lakes and gardens, as well as a fenced children's play area, skatepark, aviaries, boating lake and approach golf in Summer.

Pittville Pump Room, 01242 523852, still offers the chance to take the waters which were considered a 'cure-all' in the nineteenth century. Open Mon, Wed-Sun, 10am-4pm; special events restrict access. Closed Bank Hols. Schools **Winter.**

Wishing Fish Clock, Regent Arcade. A crowd gathers each half hour to watch this intriguing clock spring into action. The monster fish blows bubbles - catch one and make a wish.

Cheltenham (near), Crickley Hill Country Park, just off A436, 4 miles S of Cheltenham, 01452 863170. Over 140 acres of woodland and parkland on the edge of the Cotswold escarpment. There are the remains of an ancient hill fort and well-marked trails. Visitor centre, open Apr-Sept, includes a children's corner. Schools.

Cirencester, St Michael's Park, off King's Street, 01285 659182. An attractive, well-kept park with two play areas. One with swings, slides and sandpits and the other a small, rustic adventure trail. There are also tennis courts and crazy golf and, in Summer, croquet, putting and barbecues for hire.

Cirencester (near), Cotswold Water Park, Shorncote, www.waterpark.org 01285 861459. Britain's largest Water Park includes 133 lakes and the Keynes and Neigh Bridge Country Parks. Located in outstanding countryside it has nature reserves with lakeside walks, a children's beach, paddling area, cycle hire, picnic sites, cafe and gift shop. A visitor centre displays the history of the park and the conservation work. There are seasonal facilities for children's holiday activity days for which charges are made. These include many water sports (kayaking, canoeing, sailing, windsurfing, waterskiing, snorkelling and raft building), fishing, horse riding and camping. Schools Birthdays **Winter Check out 'Directory of Activities' and page 20.**

The Forest of Dean, www.forestry.gov.uk 01594 833057. In the far West of the county, between the rivers Severn and Wye, are some 30,000 acres of woodland to explore. There is a year-round programme of special events, adventure activities and many trails, tracks, cycle routes and nature reserves. The famous 4 mile Sculpture Trail – find the stained glass window or the giant fir-cone! - starts from Beechenhurst Lodge on the B4226, where there is a café, adventure play area, picnic area and information point.

> Go hiking, go walking, go cycling. Take a picnic, take a ball, take a kite.
> Use the many open spaces there are. Get a map!

Gloucester, Gloucester Cathedral, off Westgate Street, www.gloucestercathedral.uk.com 01452 528095. Find the tomb of Edward II and see where scenes from the 'Harry Potter' films were shot. A free leaflet for children brings this Norman cathedral alive. Open daily, 9am-6pm; special events restrict access. Schools **Winter**

Gloucester Park, Parkend Road. A central park, site of the fair and carnival in Summer. Bandstand, large well-equipped children's play area and skatepark.

Robinswood Hill Country Park, Reservoir Road, 01452 303206. Paths and trails criss-cross 250 acres of countryside which is perfect for walks and picnics. On site are the Rare Breeds Farm and the Gloucestershire Wildlife Trust Conservation Centre. Discovery days are held during school holidays. Schools.

St James City Farm, 23 Albany Street, Tredworth, 01452 305728. The farm offers `hands on' contact with a variety of farm animals. Animal feeding takes place throughout the day. Picnic area. Open Apr-Sept, daily, 10am-5pm; Oct-Mar, Tues-Sun, 10am-4pm. Schools **Winter.**

Westgate Leisure Area, St Oswalds Road, 01452 414100. There is a lake with canoes and paddle boats for hire, a 9 hole pitch and putt course, picnic benches and riverside walks. Open Easter-Sept.

Nympsfield (near), **Coaley Peak Picnic Site,** 2 miles N of Uley on the B4066 and just across the road from the entrance to Woodchester Mansion (check out 'Historic Sites'). This 12 acre site offers panoramic views of the Severn Vale, and adjoins a National Trust nature reserve complete with topograph.

Stroud, **The Museum in the Park,** Stratford Park, 01453 763394, is full of imaginative displays - from dinosaurs to the world's first lawnmower. Quiz trails and activity packs linking the museum to its parkland setting. Open Apr-Sept, Tues-Fri, 10am-5pm, Sat-Sun, 11am-5pm, Oct-Mar, Tues-Fri, 10am-4pm, Sat-Sun 11am-4.30pm, Bank Hols, 11am-5pm. Telephone for Dec times. Schools **Winter.**
Stratford Park. A park with woodland walks, duck pond, bandstand, children's play area, skatepark, tennis courts and, in Summer, putting. It adjoins the Leisure Centre and the Museum in the Park (check out 'Historic Sites').

Tewkesbury, **The Merchant's House (The Little Museum),** 45 Church Street, 01684 297174. A restored medieval timber-framed house. Tudor Living History days for schools. Open Apr-Oct, Tues-Sat, Bank Hols, 10am-5pm. Telephone for Winter opening. Schools **Winter.**
Tewkesbury Abbey, Church Street, www.tewkesburyabbey.org.uk 01684 850959, is an impressive building and larger than many cathedrals. There are leaflets for children, fun activities and tours by arrangement. Open daily, 7am-5pm (6pm Sat-Sun). Special events restrict access. Schools **Winter.**

Wotton-under-Edge, **Wotton Heritage Centre,** The Chipping, 01453 521541. This small, friendly Centre has a lot of information about this historic wool town and changing displays. Open Tues-Fri, 10am-1pm & 2-5pm (4pm Winter), Sat, 10am-1pm. Schools **Winter.**

WILTSHIRE

Avebury, Avebury Stone Circle, NT. The village is set within this famous megalithic stone circle. You can walk around the stones and avenue of megaliths. Car parking and picnic area outside village.

Bradford-on-Avon, Barton Farm Countryside Park. Set in the wooded valley of the River Avon, the park is flanked by the river and the Kennet and Avon Canal and has plenty of walks. There is a well-preserved Tithe Barn, a 14th century building maintained by English Heritage.
Bradford-on-Avon Museum, Bridge Street, www.bradfordmuseum.com 01225 863280, displays the heritage of the region. The centrepiece is a rebuilt 120 year old pharmacy shop. Quiz sheets available. Open Easter-Oct, Wed-Sat, 10.30am-12.30pm & 2-4pm, Sun, 2-4pm; Nov-Easter, Wed-Fri & Sun, 2-4pm, Sat 10.30am-12.30pm & 2-4pm and Bank Hol Mons 2-4pm. Schools **Winter.**

Bratton, Bratton Camp and the White Horse, EH. Pack a picnic and enjoy the views from this Iron Age Hill Fort. Take care when close to this, the oldest of Wiltshire's landmark white horses - the surface, now concrete, is extremely slippery.

Chippenham, Chippenham Museum and Heritage Centre, 10 Market Place, 01249 705020. Discover the town's rich heritage, from the Jurassic period through to the Victorians. Hear King Alfred describe Saxon life and the struggle against the Vikings. Open Mon-Sat, 10am-4pm. Schools **Winter.**
John Coles Park, Fleet Road. There are bowls, tennis courts, a fenced play area, bandstand and plenty of open space for games in this beautifully kept park.

Corsham, Heritage Centre, Arnold House, High Street, 01249 714660. Two child-friendly displays with touch-screen computers focus on the local woollen industry and stone quarrying. Open Mon-Sat, 10am-4.30pm; confirm Winter Sat opening. Schools **Winter.**

Devizes, Devizes Visitor Centre, Market Place, 01380 729408. A small interactive exhibition looks at Devizes Castle and the Civil War between Stephen and Matilda. Open Mon-Sat, 9.30am-5pm. Schools **Winter.**
Hillworth Park, has fenced play areas, space to run around, an aviary and tennis courts(walk on and play).

Devizes (near), Caen Hill Locks, off A361 W of Devizes. Walk along the towpath and discover how engineers were able to bring the Kennet and Avon Canal uphill to the town of Devizes. Visit before mid-afternoon and there might be boats negotiating the locks.

Malmesbury, Athelstan Museum, Town Hall, Cross Hayes, 01666 829258, has local history displays, coins, early bicycles and a fire pump. The children's corner has `hands on' activities including brass and fossil rubbing. Telephone for opening times. Schools **Winter.**

Marlborough (near), Savernake Forest, www.forestry.gov.uk 01594 833057. Once a royal hunting forest, there are 2,300 acres of woodland, rides and open glades, with deer still to be seen. There are plenty of walks and trails to follow.

Salisbury, Salisbury Cathedral, www.salisburycathedral.org.uk 01722 555120, is a medieval masterpiece, built in only 38 years. Follow the children's trail looking for animals and symbols or take a guided Tower Tour (age/height restrictions apply). Open daily, 7.15am-6.15pm; special events restrict access. Schools **Winter.**
Victoria Park, Castle Road. There is a large, fenced play area, tennis courts, crazy golf and a formal park area.
Winston Churchill Gardens, Southampton Road. A formal park with a lovely riverside walk. There is also a skate park, roller hockey pitch and a fenced area with play equipment for younger children.

Swindon, Coate Water Country Park, 01793 490150, surrounds a large fishing lake. There is pitch and putt, miniature golf, picnic and barbecue areas, a paddling pool, play equipment, a nature reserve with bird hides and a miniature railway(Sun & Bank Hol afternoons in Summer). Also, an exhibition about the history of Coate Water.
Lydiard Park, 01793 771419. Farmland and woodland walks, nature trails, extensive and exciting play areas for children and a visitors' centre with exhibitions. Check out 'Historic Sites'. Open daily till dusk. Schools.
Swindon Museum and Art Gallery, Bath Road, 01793 466556, houses a collection of 20th century British art and displays of local history, archaeology and geology. See the Egyptian Mummy and find a huge Gharial! Open Mon-Sat, 10am-5pm, Sun, 2-5pm. Closed Bank Hols. Schools **Winter.**

Trowbridge, Trowbridge Museum, The Shires, Court Street, www.trowbridgemuseum.co.uk 01225 751339, tells the story of a West Country woollen town. Look out for the Mouse Trail and excellent reconstructions of a weaver's cottage and Trowbridge Castle. Open Tues-Fri, 10am-4pm, Sat, 10am-5pm. Schools **Winter.**
Trowbridge Park, Park Road, is West Wiltshire's largest park. It has a popular fenced play area and a hardcourt suitable for volleyball, basketball and hockey. In Summer there is crazy golf.

Warminster, Lake Pleasure Grounds, off Weymouth Street. There is a large lake which is fed by the River Were, playground, skatepark, tennis courts, paddling pool and putting in Summer.

Wroughton (near), Barbury Castle Country Park, 01793 771419. Dramatic scenery, a hillfort and ancient trackways, including The Ridgeway National Trail, one of the oldest roads in the world. Picnic area.

This Directory covers lots of different activities to try out which may lead to new interests and hobbies. Individually or as a family you can hire bikes or boats, go bowling, ice skating or dry-slope skiing. Sport is a great way for young people to channel surplus, energy or occupy spare time. It can offer personal challenge, foster team spirit and generate an interest which can provide a pleasurable and necessary diversion in later life. Sport is a good way to have fun and make new friends; to look fit and feel good.

Be creative and try pottery painting or craft activities. Be adventurous and visit an outdoor pursuits centre to take up watersports. For a more restful time, look up the programmes at the cinema or have a treat and go to the theatre for some live performances. Many places mentioned organise special courses, workshops and activities for children all year round.

General abbreviations used in addresses within the listings are as follows: Ave:Avenue Clo:Close Cresc:Crescent Dr:Drive Gdns:Gardens Gr:Green Gro:Grove La:Lane Pde:Parade Pk:Park Pl:Place RG:Recreation Ground Rd:Road Sq:Square St:Street.

Abbreviations specific to a particular section are listed at the beginning of that section.

ADVENTURE ACTIVITIES

For water based activities check out `Watersports'.
Abbreviations: A:Archery Ab:Abseiling AC:Assault Course BB:Bridgebuilding Cl:Climbing Cv:Caving MB:Mountain Biking O:Orienteering PS:Problem Solving R:Riding RC:Ropes Course.
BRISTOL & BATH AREA: Banwell: Mendip Outdoor Pursuits 01934 820518/823666 A Ab AC Cl Cv O PS. Churchill: High Action Ltd Lyncombe Dr 01934 852335 A O R.
GLOUCESTERSHIRE: Christchurch: Forest Adventure (groups only) 01594 834661 A Ab Cl Cv MB O PS, Motiva Ropes Course 01594 861762 RC, On Target Activities 01594 860581 A. Cirencester (Cotswold Water Park): The Adventure Zone (school hols Easter-Oct) 01285 861816 A MB O R, Waterland Outdoor Pursuits (groups only) 01285 861202 A BB O **Check out page 20.** Coleford: Wyedean Canoe & Adventure Centre 01594 833238 A Ab Cl Cv O PS RC.

ADVENTURE HOLIDAYS

Camp Beaumont, www.campbeaumont.com 01603 284280, has five residential, multi-activity Summer Camps in Norfolk, the Isle of Wight, Staffordshire and the Lake District. Each one offers a huge range of over 70 exciting daytime activities including abseiling, motorsports and lazer tag and evening entertainment of games and galas. There are also specialist holidays such as 'Movie Maker', 'Wizards & Witches School', 'Watersports', 'Learner Driver', 'All Stars Football' and many more. Holidays are available for 6-10yrs, 10-13yrs and 13-16yrs, during the Easter hols and Summer hols from 12th Jul- end Aug. The holidays include full board and accommodation and are overseen by specially trained staff in safe and secure environments. Schools **Price G Check out page 20.**

BOAT HIRE

Abbreviations: C:Canoes CC:Canadian Canoes DC:Day Cruisers K:Kayaks M:Motor Boats NB:Narrow Boats P:Pedaloes Pb:Paddleboats Pn:Punts R:Rowing Boats S:Skiffs SD:Sailing Dinghies SE:Self-drive Electric Boats WB:Windsurfing Boards.
BRISTOL & BATH AREA: Bath: **Bath Boating Station** Forester Rd 01225 466407 C Pn S. Located just 10 minutes walk from the city centre, the Station has the only fleet of punts in the West Country and also the largest fleet of Thames Rowing Skiffs in England. All of these boats are period pieces and provide a delightful way of exploring this beautiful stretch of river. Tuition in poling a punt is available from the boating station staff. Open Apr-Sept, daily, 10am-6pm. Telephone for Winter opening. **Check out 'Trips' and page 43.** Bathford: on River Avon 01225 859847 C M R. Monkton Combe: on Kennet & Avon Canal 01225 722292 CC SE. Portishead: Lake Grounds C P Pb R.

GLOUCESTERSHIRE: Bredons Hardwick: 01684 772321 C SD WB. Cheltenham: Pittville Park Pb R.

Cirencester (Cotswold Water Park): Waterland 01285 861202 C K SD WB, Colin Mortimer Boat Hire 07970 419208 P R **Check out page 20.**

Gloucester: on Gloucester to Sharpness Canal 01453 882048 NB, Westgate Leisure Area St Oswalds Rd 01452 414100 C Pb. Lechlade: on River Thames 01793 700241 DC R SE, 01367 253599 M R S. Symonds Yat East: on River Wye 01594 833238 CC K. Tewkesbury: on River Avon 01684 294088 M DC.

WILTSHIRE: Bradford-on-Avon: on Kennet & Avon Canal 01225 867187 CC SE. Devizes: on Kennet & Avon Canal 01380 728504 NB. Salisbury: Millstream Approach R. Semington: on Kennet & Avon Canal 01380 870654 SE.

BOWLING (TEN PIN)

BRISTOL & BATH AREA: Bristol: Bowlplex Aspects Leisure Pk Longwell Gr 0117 9610000, Hollywood Bowl Avonmeads Retail Pk 0117 9771777, Megabowl Brunel Way Ashton Gate 0117 9538538. Weston-super-Mare: AMF Bowling Carlton St 01934 626480.
GLOUCESTERSHIRE: Cheltenham: Cotswold Bowl 2 Wymans La Kingsditch 01242 226766. Coleford: Little Follies Mile End Rd 01594 833229. Gloucester: Megabowl Centre Severn Barnwood 01452 616262, Minnesota Fats Sports Bar The Peel Centre 01452 414962.
WILTSHIRE: Melksham: Christie Miller Sports Centre 32 Lancaster Rd Bowerhill 01225 702826. Salisbury: Strikers Unit 5 Milford Trading Est Blakey Rd 01722 413121. Swindon: Megabowl Whitehill Way 01793 886886.

CINEMAS

BRISTOL & BATH AREA: Bath: ABC 23/24 Westgate St 01225 461730, Little Theatre St Michael's Pl 01225 466822, Robins Cinema St John's Pl 01225 461506. Bristol: Cineworld Hengrove 01275 831099, Cube Dove St South 0117 9074190, Imax® At-Bristol Anchor Rd 0845 3451235, Odeon* Union St, Orpheus Northumbria Dr Henleaze 0117 9621644, Showcase St Philips Causeway 0117 9723800, Warner Village Aspects Leisure Pk Longwell Gr 0870 2406020, Warner Village Cribbs Causeway 0870 2406020, Watershed Media Centre 1 Canons Rd 0117 9253845. Clevedon: Curzon Old Church Rd 01275 871000. Weston-super-Mare: Odeon* The Centre.
GLOUCESTERSHIRE: Cheltenham: Odeon* Winchcombe St. Cinderford: The Palace Belle Vue Rd 01594 822555. Cirencester: Cinema Lewis La 01285 658755. Coleford: Studio High St 01594 833331. Gloucester: New Olympus Film Theatre Barton St 01452 507549, UGC Cinemas The Peel Centre Bristol Rd 0870 1555174.
WILTSHIRE: Chippenham: Astoria Cinema Marshfield Rd 01249 652498. Devizes: Palace Cinema The Market Pl 01380 722971. Salisbury: Odeon* New Canal. Swindon: Cineworld Greenbridge Retail & Leisure Pk 01793 420710, UGC Cinemas Shaw Ridge Leisure Pk Whitehill Way 0870 1555134.

---

*ODEON CINEMAS Hotline: 0870 5050007

CLIMBING CENTRES

Also check out `Adventure Activities'.
BRISTOL & BATH AREA: Bristol: Bristol Climbing Centre Mina Rd 0117 9413489.
GLOUCESTERSHIRE: Gloucester: Warehouse Climbing Centre Parliament St 01452 302351.
WILTSHIRE: Swindon: Link Centre Whitehill Way Westlea 01793 445566. Tidworth: Leisure Centre Nadder Rd 01980 847140.

CRAZY GOLF

BRISTOL & BATH AREA: Bristol: Megabowl Brunel Way Ashton Gate (indoor) 0117 9538538. Clevedon: Salt House Fields. Weston-super-Mare: opposite Grand Pier.
GLOUCESTERSHIRE: Cirencester: St Michael's Park off King's St 01285 659182.
WILTSHIRE: Chippenham: Monkton Park 01249 653928. Salisbury: Victoria Park. Swindon: Coate Water Country Park 01793 522837. Trowbridge: Trowbridge Park.

CYCLE HIRE

BRISTOL & BATH AREA: Bath: Avon Valley Cyclery rear of Bath Spa Station 01225 461880. Bristol: Bicycle Hire & Whistle Stop Cafe Smeaton Rd 0780 3651945. Monkton Combe: Dundas Enterprises 01225 722292.
GLOUCESTERSHIRE: Bourton-on-the-Water: Hartwells Cycle Hire High St 01451 820405. Cinderford: Winner Bike Hire Forest Vale Ind Est 01594 829805. Cirencester: Go By Cycle Cotswold Water Park 07970 419208. **Check out page 20.** Cirencester: Pedal Power 5 Ashcroft Rd 01285 640505. Coleford: Pedalabikeaway Cycle Centre Cannop Valley 01594 860065. Stonehouse: Stonehouse Accessories 18 High St 01453 822881.
WILTSHIRE: Bradford-on-Avon: The Lock Inn 01225 867187. Devizes: M J Hiscock 59 Northgate St 01380 722236. Salisbury: Hayball Cycle Centre 26-30 Winchester St 01722 411378.

FAMILY RACE DAYS

Get Your Heart Racing! A family day out with a difference is a trip to the races! All racecourses offer free admission to children under 16 years, and admission for adults starts from £5 each. In addition to the excitement and colour of the racing itself, there is always plenty of additional entertainment for the children, especially at weekends and during the school holidays. To discover what exciting activities are happening near you, contact your local racecourse (details below) or log on to www.discover-racing.com where you can take advantage of advanced ticket booking offers and learn more about the sport, or call the Discover Racing Ticket Line on 08700 721 724. Check out page 16.
BATH & BRISTOL AREA: Bath: Bath Racecourse www.bath-racecourse.co.uk 01225 424609.
GLOUCESTERSHIRE: Cheltenham: Cheltenham Racecourse www.cheltenham.co.uk 01242 513014.
WILTSHIRE: Netherhampton: Salisbury Racecourse www.salisburyracecourse.co.uk 01722 326461.

HELPING GREAT ORMOND STREET

Great Ormond Street Hospital Children's Charity, www.gosh.org.uk 0207 916 5678, needs everyone's support to help raise £12 million each year. There are many ways to get involved in raising money to help buy medical equipment, fund pioneering research and provide support services for the young patients and their families. Look for and support many special events throughout the year some of which are detailed below. You can make a difference.
Write4GOSH prize giving, 14th Feb, Great Ormond Street Hospital. The winners of the first GOSH online competition will be announced by celebrity judges, headed by Cherie Booth QC.
Jeans for Genes, Fri 3rd Oct. Swap your uniform or business suit for jeans, and donate £1 to genetic research. Contact: Rachel Smith 020 7916 5678.

ICE SKATING

BRISTOL & BATH AREA: Bristol: John Nike Leisuresport Ltd Bristol Ice Rink Frogmore St 0117 9292148.
WILTSHIRE: Swindon: Link Centre Whitehill Way Westlea 01793 445566.

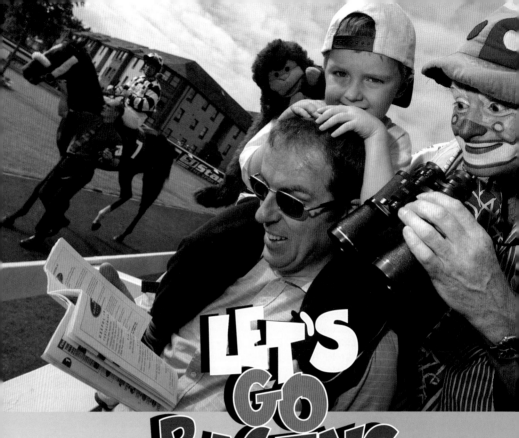

LET'S GO RACING

For a family day out with a difference, why not check out your local racecourse? In addition to the wonderful colour and excitement, there's usually loads of entertainment for kids, especially at weekends and during school holidays.

To discover racing activities near you, simply contact your local racecourse via the details in the Directory chapter of this book, or contact Discover Racing. Discover Racing provides everything you need to organise a day or night out at the races, including great ticket discounts.

DISCOVER

RACING

Kids under 16 years are admitted FREE!

Tickets & Information Call: 08700 721 724

Or Click: www.discover-racing.com

KARTING

BRISTOL & BATH AREA: Bristol: The Raceway Avonmouth Way Avonmouth 01275 817011, West Country Karting Ltd Bradley Stoke 01454 202666.
GLOUCESTERSHIRE: Gloucester: JDR Indoor Karting 5 Madleaze Ind Est Bristol Rd 01452 311211. Stroud: Aston Down Raceway Ltd Aston Down 01285 760834.
WILTSHIRE: Castle Combe: Skid Pan & Kart Track 01249 783010. Coombe Bissett: Wessex Raceway 01725 519599. Swindon: Winners Area One Hackpen La Wroughton Airfield 01793 814340. West Dean: Avago Karting 01794 884693.

LASER FUN

BRISTOL & BATH AREA: Bath: Quasar Corn St 01225 463311. Bristol: Harry's Quasar Centre All Saints St 0117 9277671.

LOCAL COUNCILS

Council Leisure departments are able to provide information on council run facilities for children.
BRISTOL & BATH AREA: Bath & North East Somerset Council 01225 477000, Bristol City Council 0117 9222000, North Somerset Council 01934 888888, South Gloucestershire Council 01454 868686.
GLOUCESTERSHIRE: **Gloucestershire County Council 01452 425000,** Cheltenham Borough Council 01242 262626, Cotswold District Council 01285 643643, Forest of Dean District Council 01594 810000, Gloucester City Council 01452 522232, Stroud District Council 01453 766321, Tewkesbury Borough Council 01684 295010.
WILTSHIRE: Wiltshire County Council 01225 713000, Kennet District Council 01380 724911, North Wiltshire District Council 01249 706111, Salisbury District Council 01722 336272, Swindon Borough Council 01793 463000, West Wiltshire District Council 01225 776655.

MAIZE MAZES

Subject to availability, please telephone before visit. Seasonal (Jul-Sept) www.maizemaze.com
BRISTOL & BATH AREA: Banwell: Court Farm Country Park Wolvershill Rd 01934 822383.
GLOUCESTERSHIRE: Chipping Campden: Hidcote Manor Farm Hidcote Bartrim 01386 430178.
WILTSHIRE: Ansty: PYO & Farm Shop 01747 829072.
Swindon: **Great Western Maize Maze,** Lower Salthrop, 1 mile S of M4 Jn16, www.greatwesternmaze.com 01793 731806. Get lost in a seven-acre puzzle carved out of a living maize crop. No need to worry though, Ronny the Runner and Maisy the Maze Master will be watching out for you, ready to point you in the right direction. There is an exciting new theme for 2003 and, of course, a totally different maze. The courtyard with its six-minute mazes and table-top puzzles offers a welcome chance to rest your legs, but keep an eye out for the tricks and water pistols of the fun-loving helpers. An amazing day out for the whole family, from toddlers in buggies to grandparents! Picnic area and light refreshments. An adult must accompany any child under 14 years. Watch the website for news of another maze opening in the Bath area. Open mid Jul-mid Sept, daily, from 10am with last admission 5pm. Schools Birthdays **Price B Check out inside back cover.**

MUSIC AND MOVEMENT

Jo Jingles, www.jojingles.co.uk 01494 719360, is a leading pre-school music and singing experience with an educational slant which runs exciting and stimulating music and movement classes for young children at venues all over the country. For details of classes in your area or for details on the franchise opportunity please call 01494 719360, email: headoffice@jojingles.co.uk or visit the website. Birthdays **Check out page 20.**

PAINT YOUR OWN POTTERY SHOPS

BRISTOL & BATH AREA: Bristol: Art 4 Fun 14 High St Westbury on Trym 0117 9507777, Kiln

Time 10 Kings Rd Clifton 0117 9095456, Make Your Mark 97 Whiteladies Rd Clifton 0117 9744257. Wickwar: English Country Pottery Ltd 01454 299100 Christmas time only.
GLOUCESTERSHIRE: Cheltenham: Paint-It-Yourself Pottery Co Winchcombe St 01242 575700. Nailsworth: Paint a Pot 5 Cossack Sq 01453 835043.
WILTSHIRE: Salisbury: Splash of Colour 72 Fisherton St 01722 322250.

PITCH AND PUTT

We include golf courses where families are welcome.
BRISTOL & BATH AREA: Bath: Approach Golf Course Western Rd 01225 331162. Bristol: Ashton Court Estate Clifton Lodge entrance 0117 9738508, Pitch & Putt Golf Course Tower Rd South Warmley 0117 9675859. Portishead: Approach Golf Course Nore Rd, Lake Grounds Park.
GLOUCESTERSHIRE: Andoversford: Shipton Golf Course 01242 890237. Cheltenham: Pittville Park 01242 528764. Gloucester: Ski & Snowboard Centre Matson La 01452 414300, Westgate Leisure Area St Oswalds Rd 01452 414100.
WILTSHIRE: Chippenham: Monkton Park 01249 653928. Highworth: Golf Centre Swindon Rd 01793 766014. Melksham: Christie Miller Sports Centre 01225 702826. Swindon: Coate Water Country Park 01793 522837.

PUTTING GREENS

BRISTOL & BATH AREA: Bath: Royal Victoria Park 01225 425066. Clevedon: Salt House Fields. Monkton Combe: Combe Grove Manor Hotel & Country Club Brassknocker Hill 01225 835533. Weston-super-Mare: Beach Lawns 01934 643510, Park House Putting 34 Knightstone Rd 01934 621170.
GLOUCESTERSHIRE: Cirencester: St Michael's Park off King's St 01285 659182. Stroud: Stratford Park 01453 766771. Tredington: Sherdon's Golf Centre 01684 274782.
WILTSHIRE: Highworth: Golf Centre Swindon Rd 01793 766014. Swindon: Coate Water Country Park 01793 522837. Warminster: Lake Pleasure Grounds.

QUAD BIKING

BRISTOL & BATH AREA: Bristol: West Country Mini Quads Bradley Stoke 01454 202666. Wellow: Trekking Centre (groups only) 01225 834376.
WILTSHIRE: Lacock: Kiddie Pursuits (groups only) 01249 730388.

SKATE PARKS

BRISTOL & BATH AREA: Bath: Royal Victoria Park. Bristol: Dame Emily Skateboard Park Bedminster, Hengrove Play Park, SK8 & Ride 74 Avon St 0117 9079995, St George Park. Keynsham: Memorial Park off High St. Thornbury: Skatepark behind Leisure Centre. Yate: Peg Hill Skatepark off Gravel Hill Rd.
GLOUCESTERSHIRE: Cheltenham: Pittville Park. Gloucester: Gloucester Park. Stroud: Stratford Park.
WILTSHIRE: Melksham: King George V Playing Field (one skate ramp). Salisbury: Winston Churchill Gardens. Warminster: Lake Pleasure Grounds.

SNOW SPORTS

BRISTOL & BATH AREA: Churchill: Avon Ski Centre Lyncombe Dr 01934 852335.
GLOUCESTERSHIRE: Gloucester: Ski & Snowboard Centre Matson La 01452 414300.

> There are a number of Brewsters Fun Factories in the area.
> Call 0845 222 800 for details.

Age and height restrictions generally apply.

BRISTOL & BATH AREA: Bath: Sports & Leisure Centre North Parade Rd 01225 462563/462565. Bristol: Alphabet Zoo Winterstoke Rd 0117 9663366, Bradley Stoke Leisure Centre Fiddlers Wood La 01454 867050, Castaways Children's Playland Waters Rd Kingswood 0117 9615115, Kingswood Leisure Centre Church Rd Staple Hill 01454 865700, Mayhem SpringHealth Leisure Club Station Rd Little Stoke 01454 888666, Planet Kids Megabowl Brunel Way Ashton Gate 0117 9538538, Wacky Warehouse The Wishing Well Aspects Leisure Pk Longwell Gr 0117 9475341, Windmill Hill City Farm Bedminster 0117 9633252. Kewstoke: The Fun Factory Old Manor Pub 01934 515143. Midsomer Norton: Panda-monium Pows Orchard 01761 419091, South Wansdyke Sports Centre Rackvernal Rd 01761 415522. Portishead: Parish Wharf Leisure Centre Harbour Rd 01275 848494. Thornbury: Leisure Centre Alveston Hill 01454 865777. Weston-super-Mare: Grand Pier 01934 620238, Kidscove Searle Cresc 01934 417411, Wacky Warehouse The Bucket & Spade Spine Rd Westwick Island 01934 521235. Yate: Leisure Centre Kennedy Way 01454 865800.

GLOUCESTERSHIRE: Bourton-on-the-Water: Fundays Bourton Ind Pk 01451 822999. Bredons Hardwick: Playzone of Tewkesbury Croft Farm 01684 773873. Cheltenham: Ballyhoo Chosen View Rd 01242 252205, Recreation Centre Tommy Taylors La 01242 528764. Coleford: Little Follies Mile End Rd 01594 833229. Gloucester: Laughter Land RAF Base Naas La Quedgeley 01452 729722, Megabowl Centre Severn Barnwood 01452 616262, PlayZone Riverside Sports & Leisure Club St Oswald's Rd 01452 413214. Stroud: Stratford Park Leisure Centre Stratford Rd 01453 766771.

WILTSHIRE: Chippenham: Pirate Pete's Playden The Millhouse Bath Rd 01249 446474. Marlborough: Leisure Centre Barton Dene 01672 513161. Melksham: Boomerang Merlin Way Bowerhill 01225 702000. Salisbury: Clown About Unit 5 Milford Trading Est Blakey Rd 01722 413121.

Swindon: **Jolly Roger Adventure,** Greenbridge Rd, www.jollyrogerplay.com 01793 522044. One of the biggest indoor play areas in the South with bouncy castles and an amazing soft and adventure play area. Children can get mangled, go for a dip in one of the seven ball pools or mess about in the biff and bash bags, webbed tunnels and `Little Tikes' area and there's much more. While the children are using up all that energy, parents can sit back, relax and enjoy a cup of tea or coffee and a snack. The whole family can stay for dinner. Then after dinner the children can go for a drive in the special driving area where they can hop on a bus, post office van or even a police car. Open daily, 9.30am-6pm. Birthdays **Winter Check out outside back cover.**

Swindon: Jungle Bungle The Village Hotel & Leisure Club Old Vicarage La 01793 833700, Oasis Leisure Centre North Star Ave 01793 445401. Tisbury: Tisbury & District Sports Centre Weaveland Rd 01747 871141. Trowbridge: Wally's Soft Play Centre 60 Shails La 01225 776799. Westbury: Jungle Jacks Headquarters Rd West Wilts Trading Est 01373 824824.

Many places in this Directory of Activities organise Birthday Parties. Give them a call.

SPORTS AND LEISURE CENTRES

Abbreviations: LC:Leisure Centre RC:Recreation Centre SC:Sports Centre SH:Sports Hall.

*:'Dual use' system, i.e. schools use the facilities but the centres are available to the general public from early evening during the week, at weekends, throughout the school holidays and, in some cases, at other times as well.

20

BRISTOL & BATH AREA: Backwell: LC Farleigh Rd 01275 463726. Bath: S & LC North Parade Rd 01225 462563/462565, Culverhay SC* Rush Hill 01225 480882, Sports Training Village University of Bath 01225 826339. Bristol: Bradley Stoke LC Fiddlers Wood La 01454 867050, Coombe Dingle Sports Complex Coombe La 0117 9626718, Downend SC* Garnett Pl 0117 9560688, Easton LC Thrissell St 0117 9558840, Filton S & LC (& Dolphin Pool) Elm Park 01454 866696, Grange SC* Tower Rd North Warmley 01454 862822, Horfield SC Dorian Rd 0117 9521650, Kingsdown SC Portland St 0117 9426582, Kingswood LC Church Rd Staple Hill 01454 865700, Patchway SC* Hempton La 01454 865890, Robin Cousins SC West Town Rd 0117 9823514, Whitchurch SC Bamfield 01275 833911. Chew Magna: Chew Valley SC* Chew La 01275 333375. Churchill: SC* Churchill Gr 01934 852303. Clevedon: Strode LC Strode Rd 01275 879242, Swiss Valley SC* Valley Rd 01275 877182. Keynsham: LC Temple St 01225 395161. Midsomer Norton: South Wansdyke SC Rackvernal Rd 01761 415522. Nailsea: Scotch Horn LC Brockway 01275 856965. Pill: St Katherine's SC* Pill Rd 01275 373287. Portishead: Gordano SC* St Mary's Rd 01275 843942, Parish Wharf LC Harbour Rd 01275 848494. Thornbury: LC Alveston Hill 01454 865777. Weston-super-Mare: Hutton Moor LC Hutton Moor Rd 01934 635347, Wyvern SC* Marchfields Way 01934 642426. Yate: LC Kennedy Way 01454 865800, Outdoor Sports Complex* next to Brimsham Green School 01454 865820.

GLOUCESTERSHIRE: Cheltenham: Bournside SC* Warden Hill Rd 01242 239123, Cleeve SC* Two Hedges Rd Bishops Cleeve 01242 673581, RC Tommy Taylors La 01242 528764, St Benedicts SC* Arle Rd 01242 226299. Chipping Campden: SC* Cidermill La 01386 841595. Cinderford: Heywood LC* Causeway Rd 01594 824008. Cirencester: Cotswold LC Tetbury Rd 01285 654057. Coleford: Five Acres LC* Berry Hill 01594 835388. Dursley: SC* Rednock Dr 01453 543832/546441. Eastcombe: Thomas Keble LC* 01452 770617. Fairford: SC* Farmors School Campus 01285 713786. Gloucester: Beaufort SC* Holmleigh Pk Tuffley 01452 303256, Brockworth SC* Mill La 01452 863518, Churchdown SC* Winston Rd 01452 855994, GL1 LC Bruton Way 01452 396666, Sir Thomas Rich's SC* Oakleaze Longlevens 01452 338439. Lydney: Whitecross LC* Church Rd 01594 842383. Nailsworth: RC* Nailsworth Primary School Nympsfield Rd 01453 836951. Newent: LC* Watery La 01531 821519. Stonehouse: Maidenhill RC* Woodcock La 01453 824366. Stroud: Archway SC* Paganhill 01453 767374, Stratford Park LC Stratford Rd 01453 766771. Tetbury: S & LC* Sir William Romney School Lowfield Rd 01666 505805. Tewkesbury: SC* Ashchurch Rd Newtown 01684 293953. Wanswell: Berkeley Vale LC* 01453 511617. Wotton-under-Edge: Wotton SC* Kingswood Rd 01453 842626.

WILTSHIRE: Amesbury: SC* Antrobus Rd 01980 622173. Calne: White Horse LC* White Horse Way 01249 814032. Chippenham: Olympiad LC Monkton Pk 01249 444144, Sheldon SH* Hardenhuish La 01249 651056. Corsham: Springfield SC Beechfield Rd 01249 712846. Cricklade: LC Stones La 01793 750011. Devizes: LC* Southbroom Rd 01380 728894. Downton: LC Wick La 01725 513668. Highworth: The Rec The Elms 01793 762602. Malmesbury: Activity Zone Bremilham Rd 01666 822533. Marlborough: LC Barton Dene 01672 513161. Melksham: Christie Miller SC 32 Lancaster Rd Bowerhill 01225 702826. Pewsey: SC* Wilcot Rd 01672 562469. Salisbury: LC The Butts Hulse Rd 01722 339996, Westwood SC* Westwood Rd 01722 329717. Stratton: Community LC Grange Dr 01793 825525. Swindon: County Ground Lifestyle Centre County Rd 01793 617782, Croft SC Marlborough La Old Town 01793 526622, Dorcan Recreation Complex* St Paul's Dr Covingham 01793 533763, Haydon Centre Thames Ave Haydon Wick 01793 706666, Link Centre Whitehill Way Westlea 01793 445566, Oasis LC North Star Ave 01793 445401. Tidworth: LC Nadder Rd 01980 847140. Tisbury: Tisbury & District SC Weaveland Rd 01747 871141. Trowbridge: SC* Frome Rd 01225 764342. Warminster: SC* Woodcock Rd 01985 212946. Westbury: Leighton RC Wellhead La 01373 824448. Wootton Bassett: Lime Kiln LC* 01793 852197. Wroughton: Ridgeway LC* Inverary Rd 01793 813280.

SWIMMING POOLS (INDOOR)

BRISTOL & BATH AREA: Bristol: Bishopsworth Pool Whitchurch Rd 0117 9640258, Bristol North Pool 98 Gloucester Rd Bishopston 0117 9243548, Bristol South Pool Dean La Bedminster

NOW AND FOREVER

The Memory Returns...

Rediscover the magic that made Andrew Lloyd Webber's *Cats*
the world's longest-running and most successful musical.

PLYMOUTH Theatre Royal	15 February - 8 March 2003	01752 267222
MANCHESTER Palace Theatre	11 March - 5 April 2003	0161 242 2524
WOLVERHAMPTON Grand Theatre	8 April - 26 April 2003	01902 429212
SUNDERLAND Empire Theatre	29 April - 17 May 2003	0191 514 2517
EDINBURGH Playhouse	20 May - 7 June 2003	0870 606 3424
BELFAST Grand Opera House	10 June - 28 June 2003	028 9024 1919

and continuing on a national tour. For further details visit our website.

www.catstour.co.uk

0117 9663131, Filwood Swimming Pool Filwood Broadway Knowle West 0117 9662823, Henbury Swimming Pool Crow La 0117 9500141, Jubilee Pool Jubilee Rd Knowle 0117 9777900, Shirehampton Pool Park Rd 0117 9031624, Speedwell Pool Whitefield Rd 0117 9674778. Paulton: Swimming Pool Plumptre Rd 01761 413644.

GLOUCESTERSHIRE: Dursley: Swimming Pool Castle St 01453 546441. Tewkesbury: Cascades Oldbury Rd 01684 293740.

WILTSHIRE: Bradford-on-Avon: Bradford Pool St Margaret's St 01225 862970. Durrington: Swimming Pool Recreation Rd 01980 594594. Melksham: Blue Pool Market Pl 01225 703525. Swindon: Health Hydro Milton Rd 01793 465630. Westbury: Swimming Pool Church St 01373 822891.

> **Many Sports and Leisure Centres have Swimming Pools too.**
> **Check them out.**

SWIMMING POOLS (OUTDOOR)

BRISTOL & BATH AREA: Portishead: Open Air Pool Esplanade Rd 01275 843454.

GLOUCESTERSHIRE: Cheltenham: Sandford Parks Lido Keynsham Rd 01242 524430. Cirencester: Open Air Swimming Pool off Cecily Hill 01285 653947. Lydney: Bathurst Outdoor Swimming Pool 01594 842625. Stroud: Stratford Park Leisure Centre Stratford Rd 01453 766771. Tetbury: Sports & Leisure Centre Sir William Romney School Lowfield Rd 01666 505805. Wotton-under-Edge: Symm La 01453 842626.

WILTSHIRE: Highworth: The Rec Outdoor Pool The Elms 01793 762602. Malmesbury: Outdoor Swimming Pool Old Alexander Rd 01666 822329. Tisbury: Outdoor Pool Weaveland Rd 01747 871180.

TENNIS CENTRES

GLOUCESTERSHIRE: Gloucester: Oxstalls Indoor Tennis Centre Plock Court Tewkesbury Rd 01452 396969.

WILTSHIRE: Swindon: Delta Tennis Centre Welton Rd Westlea 01793 445555.

THEATRES

CATS on Tour, www.catstour.co.uk The longest-running musical in British theatre history has left London and is now touring the country and may be at a theatre near you! Combining the exhilarating music of Andrew Lloyd Webber, spellbinding tales from TS Eliot's 'Old Possum's Book of Practical Cats' and some of the most exciting choreography ever seen on stage, CATS really is a brilliant way to introduce children to theatre for a memory that will last forever. Get to know the playful Rum Tug Tugger, the glamorous Grizabella, the villainous Macavity, Gus, the theatre cat and the rest of the characters at one of the many local theatres on the tour. **Check out page 22.**

BRISTOL & BATH AREA: Bath: Rondo Theatre St Saviour's Rd Larkhall 01225 463362, Theatre Royal Sawclose 01225 448844. Bristol: Arnolfini 16 Narrow Quay 0117 9299191, Colston Hall Colston St 0117 9223683, Hippodrome St Augustine's Pd 0870 6077500, Old Vic King St 0117 9877877, QEH Theatre Jacob's Wells Rd 0117 9250551, Redgrave Percival Rd Clifton 0117 3157600, Ridings Arts Centre High St Winterbourne 0117 9568812, St George's Great George St 0117 9230359, Tobacco Factory Raleigh Rd Southville 0117 9020344. Weston-super-Mare: Playhouse High St 01934 645544.

GLOUCESTERSHIRE: Cheltenham: Bacon Theatre Hatherley Rd 01242 258002, Everyman Regent St 01242 572573, Playhouse Bath Rd 01242 522852. Cirencester: Brewery Arts Brewery Court 01285 655522, Sundial Theatre Cirencester College 01285 654228. Coleford: Royal Forest of Dean College Theatre Five Acres Campus Berry Hill 01594 833416. Gloucester: Guildhall Arts Centre 23 Eastgate St 01452 505089, King's Theatre Kingsbarton St 01452 300130, New

Olympus Theatre 162-166 Barton St 01452 525917. Stroud: Cotswold Playhouse Parliament St 01453 756379. Tewkesbury: Roses Theatre Sun St 01684 295074. Uley: Prema Arts Centre South St 01453 860703.
WILTSHIRE: Devizes: Wharf Theatre 01380 725944. Salisbury: Arts Centre Bedwin St 01722 321744, City Hall Malthouse La 01722 327676, Playhouse Malthouse La 01722 320333, Studio Theatre Ashley Rd 01722 336092. Swindon: Arts Centre Devizes Rd 01793 614837, Wyvern Theatre Theatre Sq 01793 524481. Trowbridge: Arc Theatre College Rd 01225 756376. Warminster: Athenaeum Centre High St 01985 213891.

TOURIST INFORMATION CENTRES

BRISTOL & BATH AREA: Bath: 01225 477101. Bristol: 0117 9260767. Gordano: 0906 8020806. Thornbury: 01454 281638. Weston-super-Mare: 01934 888800.
GLOUCESTERSHIRE: Bourton-on-the-Water: 01451 820211. Cheltenham: 01242 522878. Chipping Campden: 01386 841206. Cirencester: 01285 654180. Coleford: 01594 812388. Gloucester: 01452 396572. Moreton-in-Marsh: 01608 650881. Newent: 01531 822468. Stow on the Wold: 01451 831082. Stroud: 01453 760960. Tetbury: 01666 503552. Tewkesbury: 01684 295027.
WILTSHIRE: Amesbury: 01980 622833. Avebury: 01672 539425. Bradford-on-Avon: 01225 865797. Chippenham: 01249 706333. Corsham: 01249 714660. Devizes: 01380 729408. Malmesbury: 01666 823748. Marlborough: 01672 513989. Melksham: 01225 707424. Mere: 01747 861211. Salisbury: 01722 334956. Swindon: 01793 530328. Trowbridge: 01225 777054. Warminster: 01985 218548. Westbury: 01373 827158.

WATER FUN PARKS

Centres with some wonderful features, maybe flumes, wave machines or rapids!
GLOUCESTERSHIRE: Tewkesbury: Cascades Oldbury Rd 01684 293740.
WILTSHIRE: Chippenham: Olympiad Leisure Centre Monkton Pk 01249 444144. Swindon: Oasis Leisure Centre North Star Ave 01793 445401.

WATERSPORTS

Abbreviations: Ba:Banana Boats C:Canoeing K:Kayaking RB:Raft Building Ri:Ringos S:Sailing Sn:Snorkelling W:Windsurfing Wb:Wakeboarding Ws:Waterskiing.
BRISTOL & BATH AREA: Banwell: Mendip Outdoor Pursuits 01934 820518/823666 C K RB.
GLOUCESTERSHIRE: Bredons Hardwick: Croft Farm Leisure & Water Park 01684 772321 C S W. Christchurch: Forest Adventure (groups only) 01594 834661 C K RB, On Target Activities 01594 860581 C K.
Cirencester (Cotswold Water Park): The Adventure Zone (school hols Easter-Oct) 01285 861816 Ba C K RB Ri S W Ws, Craig Cohoon Waterski School 01285 713735 Ba Ri Wb Ws, South Cerney Outdoor Education Centre 01285 860388 C K S Sn W, Waterland Outdoor Pursuits 01285 861202 C K S RB W, Watermark Club 01285 860606 Ba Ri Ws. **Check out page 20.**
Coleford: Wyedean Canoe & Adventure Centre 01594 833238 C K RB.

YOUTH HOSTELLING

Introduce children to Youth Hostels and they will thank you when they are older! With over 200 Youth Hostels, many with family rooms, they provide a great choice for affordable family holidays in England and Wales. You can self-cater or be cooked for, stay for one night or as long as you like; youth hostelling offers flexibility and choice. Call 0870 770 8868 and ask for a family welcome pack quoting "Let's Go". **Check out page 20.**

A chance to step back in time or to step into our technological future. Art, history, science and technology find a place here.

BRISTOL AND BATH AREA

Banwell, The British Bear Collection, Banwell Castle, www.banwellcastle.co.uk 01934 822263. Teddy bears of all shapes, sizes and colours. Lots of facts about the history of bear-making and a memorable musical rendition! Open Summer, daily, 11am-5pm, Winter, Sat-Sun. Schools **Winter** Price A.

Bath, Bath Aqua Theatre of Glass, 105-107 Walcot Street, www.bathaquaglass.com 01225 428146. Demonstrations of free glass-blowing and stained glass making are held throughout the day. There are activity tables for children and a Glass Museum. Open daily, 10am-1pm, 2-5pm. Schools **Winter** Price A.

Bath Postal Museum, 8 Broad Street, www.bathpostalmuseum.org 01225 460333. Follow the history of written communication since 2000 BC in the building from which the first postage stamp was sent. Videos, computer games and quiz sheets. Open Mon-Sat, 11am-5pm, check for Jan opening. Schools **Winter** Price A.

Building of Bath Museum, The Paragon, www.bath-preservation-trust.org.uk 01225 333895, shows how the Georgians built and lived in the city. Touch screen computer and models including one of the entire city with push button illumination. Open mid Feb-end Nov, Tues-Sun & Bank Hol Mons, 10.30am-5pm. Schools Price A.

Holburne Museum of Art, Great Pulteney Street, 01225 466669, is a relatively small museum, based upon a personal collection: everything from porcelain to paintings. Activity sheets and holiday activities. Open mid Feb-end Nov, Tues-Sat, 10am-5pm, Sun, 2.30-5.30pm. Christmas art activities in Dec. Schools Price A.

Jane Austen Centre, 40 Gay Street, www.janeausten.co.uk 01225 443000. Learn about the author, her family, life in Regency Bath and the locations which feature in her novels. Quiz sheets for children. Open Mon-Sat, 10am-5.30pm, Sun, 10.30am-5.30pm. Schools **Winter** Price B.

Museum of Bath at Work, Julian Road, www.bath-at-work.org.uk 01225 318348. Enter the world of Victorian entrepreneur Mr. Bowler, whose business interests included an engineering works and a soda water business. Displays of other local industries. Open Easter-Oct, daily, 10am-5pm, Nov-Easter, Sat-Sun. Also for groups by arrangement. Schools **Winter** Price A.

Museum of Costume, Assembly Rooms, Bennett Street, www.museumofcostume.co.uk 01225 477785. Tableaux of dressed figures bring 400 years of fashion and social history vividly to life. An exhibition, 'Modern Times', covering dress in the 1920s will run until Nov 2003. Open daily, 10am-5pm. Ⓕ to BANES residents. Schools **Winter** Price B.

Museum of East Asian Art, 12 Bennett Street, www.east-asian-art.co.uk 01225 464640, provides activity packs and during the school holidays there are special art-based activity sessions. Try making a dragon-bowl, opera mask or kite. Open Tues-Sat, 10am-5pm, Sun, 12noon-5pm. Schools **Winter** Price A.

Roman Baths and Pump Room, Stall Street, www.romanbaths.co.uk 01225 477785. Follow in the footsteps of the Romans and explore the only hot spring baths in Britain, largely unchanged since Roman times. Time your visit carefully as it is always busy. Personal audio tours and regular guided tours. Open daily, Jan-Feb, 9.30am-5.30pm, Mar-Jun, 9am-6pm, Jul-Aug, 9am-10pm, Sept-Oct, 9am-6pm and Nov-Dec, 9.30am-5.30pm. Free to BANES residents. Schools **Winter** Price C.

William Herschel Museum, 19 New King Street, www.bath-preservation-trust.org.uk 01225 311342. This Georgian house contains a Star Vault and displays covering astronomy, social history, science and music. Holiday activities. Open Mon-Fri, 2-5pm, Sat-Sun, 11am-5pm. Schools **Winter Price A.**

Bath (near), American Museum, Claverton Manor, www.americanmuseum.org 01225 460503. Completely furnished rooms show how Americans lived from the 17th to 19th centuries. Look out for the Indian tepee and covered wagon. Special guide book for children. Open 22nd Mar-2nd Nov, Tues-Sun, afternoons, times vary; 22nd Nov-14th Dec for Christmas season. Reduced admission for grounds and galleries only. Schools **Price B.**

Bristol, At-Bristol, Anchor Road, Harbourside, www.at-bristol.org.uk 0845 3451235, is entertaining, educational and full of interactive displays and `hands on' activities. The main attractions of this award-winning complex can be visited separately or combination tickets are available. Open daily, 10am-6pm, Imax® also open Thurs-Sun evenings.

> **Explore@Bristol** is a comprehensive science centre. A chance to read the news in a TV studio, experiment with mirrors, build a bridge or try out the Human Hamster Wheel! Schools Birthdays **Winter Price C.**

> **Imax® Theatre@Bristol** makes the audience feel part of the action with a screen which is four storeys high and digital surround sound.

> **Wildwalk@Bristol.** An exciting exhibition of the natural world. Check out `Farms'.

British Empire and Commonwealth Museum, Temple Meads, www.empiremuseum.co.uk 0117 9254980, is an exciting new national museum, focusing on five hundred years of history, from Cabot's voyage to the return of Hong Kong. Extensive education programme. Open daily, 10am-5pm. Schools **Winter Price B.**

Clifton Observatory and Cave, 0117 9741242. Visit on a bright day to see the spectacular panorama outside projected onto a screen by the 'camera obscura'. Down a long, narrow flight of steps is a cave and viewing platform (minimum age for visiting the cave is 4). Open Summer, Mon-Fri, 11.30am-5pm, Sat-Sun, 10.30am-5pm, Winter, opens 12.30pm. Schools **Winter Price A.**

Clifton Suspension Bridge Visitor Centre, Bridge House, Sion Place, www.clifton-suspension-bridge.org.uk 0117 974 4664, uncovers the story behind Bristol's famous bridge and how it works. Displays include a four metre long interactive model. Open Apr-beg Sept, daily, 10am-5pm, check for Winter opening. Schools **Price A.**

SS Great Britain, Great Western Dock, www.ss-great-britain.com 0117 9260680. Brunel's great ship, the forerunner to all great passenger liners, is being restored to her original splendour. Included is admission to the Maritime Heritage Centre and, when moored on site, to the Matthew replica. Open daily, 10am-5.30pm (4.30pm Nov-Mar). Schools Birthdays **Winter Price B.**

National Trust : www.nationaltrust.org.uk

Dyrham, Dyrham Park, NT, 0117 9372501. This William and Mary house is approached through ancient parkland which is ideal for picnics. Family events held throughout the year. Reduced admission for Park only. House open 28th Mar-2nd Nov, Fri-Tues, 12noon-5.15pm. Park open daily, all year, 11am-5.30pm (or dusk if earlier). Closed 4th-7th Jul. Schools **Price B.**

Radstock, Midsomer Norton and District Museum, Market Hall, www.radstockmuseum.co.uk 01761 437722, houses displays depicting Victorian life and the North Somerset Coalfield, including a reconstructed coal face. See what school was like! Open Feb-Nov, Tues-Fri, Sun & Bank Hol Mons, 2-5pm, Sat, 11am-5pm. Schools **Price A.**

Weston-super-Mare, The Great Weston Train Experience, Clifton Road, www.modelmasters.co.uk 01934 629717. A European model railway exhibition at the back of a shop. Wonderful detail in scenes which range from a modern city station to snow covered mountains. Telephone for opening times. Schools **Price A.**

Helicopter Museum, Locking Moor Road, www.helicoptermuseum.co.uk 01934 635227. Visit the world's largest helicopter museum with over 60 helicopters and autogyros. Open Cockpit Days and pleasure flights available. Play area. Open Wed-Sun, 10am-6pm (4pm Nov-Mar), also Bank Hols & daily during Easter & Summer school hols. Schools **Winter Price B.**

Heritage Centre, Wadham Street, 01934 412144. The story of the town, the sea and the countryside is told with models, pictures and photographs. Open Mon-Sat, 10am-5pm but closed Bank Hols. Schools **Winter Price A.**

North Somerset Museum, Burlington Street, www.n-somerset.gov.uk/museum 01934 621028, has displays of local and natural history. Visit Clara's cottage and follow the trail, stamping your card as you go. Special exhibitions and events. Open Mon-Sat, 10am-4.30pm. Schools **Winter Price A.**

GLOUCESTERSHIRE

Berkeley, Berkeley Castle, 01453 810332. Wander through England's oldest inhabited castle or take a one-hour guided tour. Highlights are the massive Norman Keep with Dungeon and the cell where Edward II was murdered. Open 1st Apr-end Sept, Wed-Sat, 11am-4pm, Sun, 2-5pm, Bank Hol Mons, 11am-5pm; Oct, Sun, 2-5pm. Schools **Price B.**

Jenner Museum, www.jennermuseum.com 01453 810631. Find out what Dr Edward Jenner discovered about hedgehogs, cuckoos, fossils and bird migration and how his experiment (involving a cow, a milkmaid and a small boy) led to the elimination of smallpox. Open Apr-Sept, Tues-Sat & Bank Hol Mons, 12.30-5.30pm, Sun, 1-5.30pm; Oct, Sun, 1-5.30pm. Schools **Price A.**

Bibury, Arlington Mill Museum, 01285 740368, demonstrates the potential of cogs, wheels, pulleys and water-power. See machinery and learn about the Victorian way of life. Open daily, 10am-6pm (5pm Winter). Schools **Winter Price A.**

Bourton-on-the-Water, Bourton Model Railway Exhibition, Box Bush, High Street, www.bourtonmodelrailway.co.uk 01451 820686. The 00/H0 and N gauge railways run through wonderfully detailed background scenery. Press the buttons and watch them come to life. Open Apr-Sept, daily, 11am-5pm, Oct-Mar, Sat-Sun. Limited opening in Jan. Schools **Winter Price A.**

Cotswold Motoring Museum and Toy Collection, 01451 821255, is re-opening on 11th Feb with some exciting changes in displays and exhibits including a new 'Collectors Room' and a fully refurbished new shop. Housing a varied collection of cars, motorcycles, pedal cars and motoring memorabilia, look out for the little yellow car 'Brum', star of the children's TV series. For the very first time this year the Motorhouse will be open housing a 'Country Garage' exhibition and the Blacksmith's collection. Open Feb-Nov, daily, 10am-6pm. Schools Price A. **Check out page 48.**

Dragonfly Maze, Rissington Road, 01451 822251. An amazing rebus puzzle maze with clues to solve as you wander through the quarter mile of twisting pathways. Open daily, 10am-5.30pm (5pm Winter), Jan-Feb times may vary. Schools **Winter Price A.**

Miniature World, Village Green, 01451 810121. Step into the world of miniature and marvel at the time and patience that has gone into over 50 exhibits. Miniature ghosts appear and disappear before your very eyes in haunted scenes. Open Mar-Oct, daily, 10am-5.30pm, Nov-Feb, Sat-Sun. Schools **Winter Price A.**

Model Village, The Old New Inn, www.theoldnewinn.co.uk 01451 820467, is a 1/9 scale replica of Bourton-on-the-Water built in Cotswold stone, complete with the model of the model village and singing from the church. Open daily, Summer, 9am-5.45pm, Winter, 10am-3.45pm. Schools **Winter Price A.**

Perfumery Exhibition, Victoria Street, www.cotswold-perfumery.co.uk 01451 820698. There are smells to identify, a 'smelly-vision' cinema and an enchanting perfume garden. More interesting for older children. Open Mon-Sat, 9.30am-5pm, Sun, 10.30am-5pm. Schools **Winter Price A.**

Broadway (near), Snowshill Manor, NT, 01386 852410. This Cotswold Manor house is home to an amazing collection, ranging from dolls' houses and bicycles to Japanese Samurai armour. Open 29th Mar-2nd Nov, Wed-Sun (also Mon in Jul & Aug), Bank Hol Mons, 12noon-5pm. Grounds open 11am-5.30pm. Schools Price B.

Cheltenham, Holst Birthplace Museum, 4 Clarence Road, www.holstmuseum.org.uk 01242 524846. Learn how the Victorians lived: from toys in the nursery upstairs to the kitchen and scullery downstairs. Guided tours by appointment. Open Tues-Sat, 10am-4pm. Closed Dec-Jan except for pre-booked groups. Schools Price A.

Cinderford (near), Dean Heritage Centre, Soudley, www.deanmuse.co.uk 01594 822170, is planning to reopen in April 2003 following major refurbishment. Discover the story of the Forest of Dean. There are museum displays, a Victorian Forester's cottage, demonstration charcoal stack and adventure playground. Open daily, 10am-6pm (closes earlier in Winter). Schools Winter Price B.

Cirencester, Corinium Museum, Park Street, www.cotswold.gov.uk/museum 01285 655611, is closed during 2003 for refurbishment.

Coleford, Great Western Railway Museum, in main free car park, 01594 833569/832032. A small museum where you can find locomotives (model and one life-size static) and a working signal box. Miniature train rides. Open Sat, 2.30-5pm, and by arrangement. Schools Birthdays Winter Price A.

Coleford (near), Clearwell Caves, www.clearwellcaves.com 01594 832535, is an extensive natural cave system which was mined for its iron ore. See pick marks on the walls and learn about Free Mining. Deep level trips available. Dress sensibly! Open Mar-Oct, daily, 10am-5pm, Nov-Feb, Sat-Sun. Christmas Fantasy in Dec. Schools Birthdays Winter Price B.

Hopewell Colliery, Cannop Hill, 01594 810706. A true 'Free Mine' with regular underground tours. Hard hats with torches are worn. Small exhibition (free admission) and train rides. Open Easter-Oct, daily, 10am-4pm (last tour 3.15pm). Also for 'Christmas Underground'. Schools Birthdays Price B.

Gloucester, Gloucester City Museum and Art Gallery, Brunswick Road, 01452 396131. Discover dinosaurs, fossils, Roman remains, paintings and decorative arts. `Hands on' displays and children's holiday activities. Open Tues-Sat, 10am-5pm. Glos City residents & under 18s Free. Schools Winter Price A.

Gloucester Folk Museum, 99-103 Westgate Street, 01452 396467. More than three floors on local history and crafts, including a Victorian schoolroom. Try out interactive computer quizzes and `hands on' activities. Enquire about the associated Gloucester Transport Museum. Open Tues-Sat, 10am-5pm. Glos City residents & under 18s Free. Schools Winter Price A.

House of the Tailor of Gloucester, 9 College Court, 01452 422856, is a shop with a definitive range of Beatrix Potter merchandise and a small display of pictures and models. Children can view videos. Open Mon-Sat, 10am-5pm (4pm Nov-Mar). Closed Bank Hols. Under 12s Free. Schools Winter Price A.

National Waterways Museum, Llanthony Warehouse, Gloucester Docks, www.nwm.org.uk 01452 318200. An award-winning museum where interactive displays and working models follow the story of the waterways and of the people who built and used them. Explore the historic boats moored alongside or take a boat trip (check out 'Trips' chapter). Open daily, 10am-5pm. Schools Winter Price B.

Soldiers of Gloucestershire Museum, Custom House, The Docks, www.glosters.org.uk 01452 522682. Audio and visual displays portray the life of the Glosters over the last 300 years. Discover what it was like in a First World War trench at this award-winning museum. Open Apr-Oct, daily, 10am-5pm, Nov-Mar, Tues-Sun. Schools Winter Price B.

Moreton-in-Marsh, Wellington Aviation Museum, www.wellingtonaviation.org 01608 650323, is a small tribute museum and art gallery, featuring the Vickers-Armstrong Wellington bomber and Royal Air Force artefacts. Open Tues-Sun, 10am-12.30pm, 2-5pm. **Winter** Price A.

Newent, Shambles Museum, Church Street, 01531 822144. Leave modern Newent and enter a small Victorian country town. Look out for the taxidermist's and chemist's shops, complete with glass eyes! Open Mar-Oct, Tues-Sun & Bank Hol Mons, 10am-5pm (or dusk if earlier), Nov-Dec, Sat-Sun. Schools **Price B.**

Northleach, Keith Harding's World of Mechanical Music, High Street, www.mechanicalmusic.co.uk 01451 860181. Amazing self-playing musical instruments, beautiful clocks, musical boxes and automata are all displayed. Guided tours with live entertainment. Open daily, 10am-6pm. Schools **Winter** Price B.

Nympsfield (near), Woodchester Mansion, 2 miles N of Uley off the B4066, www.woodchestermansion.org.uk 01453 750455. This beautiful mansion was abandoned inexplicably before completion. Find doors that lead nowhere and watch the bats on live CCTV. Open Easter-end Sept, Sun and 1st Sat every month (every Sat, Jul-Aug), Bank Hol weekends(Sat-Mon), 11am-last tour 4pm. Schools Price A.

Stow-on-the-Wold, Toy and Collectors Museum, Park Street, www.thetoymuseum.co.uk 01451 830159. Three fascinating rooms full of Edwardian, Victorian and later toys: dolls, teddy bears, baby plates, trains, soldiers and more. Open Jun-Apr, Wed-Sat, 10am-1pm, 2-4.30pm but please check before visiting. Schools Price A.

Tewkesbury, The John Moore Countryside Museum, 41 Church Street, www.gloster.demon.co.uk 01684 297174. Learn about conservation and British wildlife. There is a collection of preserved mammals and birds. What does a fox's brush feel like? Open Apr-Oct, Tues-Sat & Bank Hol Mons, 10am-1pm, 2-5pm. Telephone for Winter opening. Schools **Winter** Price A.
Tewkesbury Museum, 64 Barton Street, 01684 295027. A small museum displaying the local history of Tewkesbury and surrounds. Have a look at the model of the Battle of Tewkesbury. Open Mon-Sat, 10am-4pm. Schools **Winter** Price A.

Twigworth, Nature in Art, 2 miles N of Gloucester, www.nature-in-art.org.uk 01452 731422. This unique museum is dedicated to art inspired by nature. Outdoor animal sculptures and play area. Children's activity days. Open Tues-Sun & Bank Hols, 10am-5pm. Schools Birthdays **Winter** Price B.

Winchcombe, Folk and Police Museum, Old Town Hall, www.winchcombemuseum.org.uk 01242 609151, houses a collection of police uniform and equipment from around the world and displays on local heritage and industries. Free activity sheets. Open Apr-Oct, Mon-Sat, 10am-4.30pm, and by arrangement for groups. Schools **Price A.**
Sudeley Castle, www.sudeleycastle.co.uk 01242 602308, is running an exhibition of Tudor costume during 2003. Look out for Charles I's bed and Katherine Parr's prayer book. There are extensive gardens and grounds, a picnic area and large adventure playground centred around a fort. Open daily, 29th Mar-2nd Nov. Castle, 11am-5pm, grounds, 10.30am-5.30pm. Gardens and grounds only, open from 1st Mar. Schools **Price B.**
Winchcombe Railway Museum, Gloucester Street, 01242 602257. Try being a signalman or clip your own ticket in the booking office! This is a `hands on' museum set within a half acre garden. Open Easter-Oct, Wed-Sun, 1.30-5pm, and daily in Aug. Schools Price A.

Winchcombe (near), Hailes Abbey, EH, off B4362, 01242 602398. Older children can take a free self-guided audio tour around the ruins of this 13th century abbey while younger children simply explore. Open Apr-Oct, daily, 10am-6pm (5pm Oct). Educational groups Free. Schools **Price A.**

The National Trust

Chedworth Roman Villa
Yanworth, Cheltenham
Tel: 01242 890256

One of the best exposed Romano-
British villa sites in Britain. The
site includes a water shrine, two bath
houses and 4th century mosaics.

Open 1st Mar - 30th Mar, Tues-Sun, 11am-4pm
26th Apr - 26th Oct, Tues-Sun, 10am-5pm
28th Oct - 16th Nov, Tues-Sun, 11am-4pm
including Bank Holidays

*Admission: Adult £3.90, Child £2.00,
Family £9.80*

Yanworth, **Chedworth Roman Villa,** NT, 8 miles SE of Cheltenham, 01242 890256. These are the remains of one of the best exposed Romano-British villas in Britain. See the ruins of this 1600 year old 'stately home' and imagine yourself back in the 4th century. As you look at the surviving mosaics, the hypocausts (Roman under floor central heating), water shrine and the many objects in the site museum, you can get a flavour of life when Britain was part of the Roman Empire. There is an audio tour and programme of Special Events throughout the year. Open Mar-Nov, Tues-Sun & Bank Hols; Mar, 11am-4pm, 1st Apr-26th Oct, 10am-5pm, 28th Oct-16th Nov, 11am-4pm. Schools Price A **Check out page 30.**

WILTSHIRE

Amesbury (near), Stonehenge, EH, 01980 624715. Perpetual mystery surrounds these famous stones on Salisbury Plain. Walk a complete circuit of the Stones. Open daily, times vary. Schools **Winter** Price B.

Avebury, Alexander Keiller Museum, NT, 01672 539250. The museum describes the life of Neolithic man in the area. See tools, skeletons and a prehistoric child called Charlie. Ticket also covers admission to an interactive exhibition in the Barn Gallery. Open daily, 10am-6pm (4pm Nov-Mar). Educational groups free by arrangement. Schools **Winter** Price A.

Calne, Atwell-Wilson Motor Museum, Stockley Lane, www.atwell-wilson.org 01249 813119. Many famous names of motoring in this small collection of vintage and classic cars, many still in use. There is also a grass play area with traditional equipment. Open Sun-Thurs & Good Fri, 11am-5pm (4pm Nov-Mar). Schools **Winter** Price A.

Calne (near), Bowood House and Gardens, www.bowood.org 01249 812102. A magnificent 18th century house with elegant rooms containing a wonderful collection of family heirlooms, built up over 250 years. These include paintings, porcelain, silver and such treasures as Queen Victoria's wedding chair, Napoleon's death mask, Lord Byron's Albanian soldier's costume and much more. Interesting rooms include Robert Adam's famous Library, Dr. Joseph Priestley's Laboratory where he discovered oxygen gas in 1774 and the Chapel. The surrounding Pleasure Grounds have lots to interest children including an extensive adventure playground and soft play palace. Open 1st Apr-2nd Nov, daily, 11am-6pm or dusk if earlier. Birthdays Price B **Check out 'Farms' and page 33.**

Crofton, Crofton Beam Engines, beside the Kennet and Avon Canal, SE of Marlborough, 01672 870300. The pumping station houses two early beam engines. Open Easter-Sept, daily, 10.30am-5pm. For 'Steam Days' please telephone. Schools Price A.

Devizes, Kennet and Avon Canal Trust Museum, The Wharf, www.katrust.org 01380 721279. With the aid of interactive video displays and models, this award winning museum tells the story of the creation and restoration of the canal. Open Mar-mid Dec, daily, 10am-5pm (4pm Winter). Schools Price A.
Wiltshire Heritage Museum, 41 Long Street, www.wiltshireheritage.org.uk 01380 727369. See collections of archaeology, social and natural history and art. `Hands on' activities include brass rubbing and dressing up. Open Mon-Sat, 10am-5pm, Sun, 12noon-4pm. Closed most Bank Hols. Mons & Suns Ⓕ. Under 17 years Ⓕ. Schools **Winter** Price A.

Lacock, Fox Talbot Museum of Photography and Lacock Abbey, NT, 01249 730459. The Museum commemorates the life and work of the 'Father of Modern Photography' and the Abbey cloisters were used as a location in the Harry Potter films. Special events programme. Museum, Abbey Grounds & Cloisters open mid Mar-beg Nov, daily, 11am-5.30pm. Museum also open Winter, Sat-Sun. Abbey open end Mar-beg Nov, Mon & Wed-Sun, 1-5.30pm. Closed Good Fri. Schools Price B.

Salisbury, Discover Salisbury, at The Medieval Hall, The Close, 01722 324731. A 40 minute big screen presentation describes Salisbury's past and the city and local area as it is today. Open Apr-Sept, daily (telephone to confirm) and all year for pre-booked groups. Schools **Price A.**

Mompesson House, NT, The Close, 01722 335659. An early 18th century house, with beautiful interiors. There is a children's guide with quiz. Open 24th Mar-28th Sept, Sat-Wed, 11am-5pm. Schools **Price A.**

Old Sarum, EH, 01722 335398. Originally a huge Iron Age Hill Fort, the ruins leave plenty of room for the imagination. Special Events during the year. Open daily, Nov-Mar 10am-4pm, Apr-Aug 9am-6pm, Sept 10am-6pm, Oct 10am-5pm. Schools **Winter Price A.**

Redcoats in The Wardrobe, 58 The Close, www.thewardrobe.org.uk 01722 414536, houses the Berkshire and Wiltshire collections of the Regiment, telling the story of global exploits spanning two and a half centuries. Beautiful gardens. Open Apr-Oct, daily, 10am-5pm & Nov, Feb, Mar, Tues-Sun. Schools **Price A.**

Salisbury and South Wiltshire Museum, The King's House, 65 The Close, www.salisburymuseum.org.uk 01722 332151. Imaginative displays cover prehistory, Old Sarum, Romans, Saxons and local history. Try out the interactive exhibits in the redesigned Stonehenge Gallery. Open Mon-Sat, 10am-5pm, also Jul-Aug only, Suns, 2-5pm. Schools **Winter Price A.**

Stourton, Stourhead House and Garden, NT, 01747 841152. Explore the fascinating temples, grottoes and lakes of the landscaped gardens and then the elegant Palladian house. Children's guidebook and regular family events. House & Garden open 28th Mar-31st Oct, Fri-Tues, 11am-5pm (or dusk if earlier). Garden (reduced admission) open daily, 9am-7pm (or dusk if earlier). Schools **Price C.**

Swindon, Lydiard House and Park, Lydiard Tregoze, 01793 770401. An 18th century house containing fine furniture and family portraits of the St. John family and surrounded by a beautiful park with walks and play areas. Open Summer, Mon-Sat, 10am-5pm, Sun 2-5pm (4pm Winter). Closed Good Fri. House closes 1pm on second Sat in May. Schools **Winter Price A.**

STEAM - Museum of the Great Western Railway, Kemble Drive, www.steam-museum.org.uk 01793 466646. What was life like in the age of steam? Film footage, `hands on' displays, reconstructions and locomotives recreate the past at this award-winning museum. Open Apr-Oct, Mon-Sat, 10am-5.30pm, Sun, 11am-5.30pm, Nov-Mar, closes 5pm. Schools Birthdays **Winter Price B.**

Tisbury (near), Old Wardour Castle, EH, 01747 870487. A picture book setting with plenty of scope for pretend play. Ring for details of Special Events. Educational groups free if pre-booked. Open Apr-Oct, daily, 10am-6pm (5pm Oct); Nov-Mar, Wed-Sun, 10am-4pm. Schools **Winter Price A.**

English Heritage:
www.english-heritage.org.uk

Warminster, Longleat House, off A36, on A362 Warminster to Frome road, www.longleat.co.uk 01985 844400. Widely regarded as one of the most beautiful stately homes open to the public and the best example of Elizabethan architecture, Longleat House is home to the 7th Marquess of Bath. Substantially completed by 1580, the House incorporates many treasures including fine French tapestries, exquisite ceilings and paintings. The Longleat Passport also includes access to Longleat Safari Park, and many more attractions. House open: weekends only, 1st Jan-4th Apr; daily, 5th Apr-24th Dec, 26th-31st Dec. All attractions open daily, 5th Apr-2nd Nov. Schools Birthdays **Winter Price G Check out 'Farms' chapter and page 33.**

Wilton (near Pewsey), Wilton Windmill, off A338 E of Pewsey, www.wiltonwindmill.co.uk 01672 870202. Join a guided tour, climb the steep staircases and find out how a windmill works.

More suitable for older children. No milling whilst open to the public. Open Easter-Sept, Suns & Bank Hol Mons, 2-5pm, also for groups by arrangement. Schools **Price A.**

Wilton (near Salisbury), Wilton Carpet Factory, Minster Street, 01722 744919. An opportunity to tour a modern working factory, see the looms in action and find out how carpets are made. A museum on site shows the history of Wilton. Telephone for factory tour information. Schools **Winter Price A/B.**

Wilton House, www.wiltonhouse.com 01722 746729, has 450 years of fascinating history and a fine art collection. Step back in time in the Tudor Kitchen and Victorian Laundry. Quiz sheets, landscaped parkland and a massive adventure playground. Open 11th Apr-27th Oct, daily, 10.30am-5.30pm. Schools Birthdays **Price C.**

Take a look in the Free Places chapter for other sites of historic interest.
Many museums have free admission.

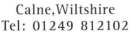

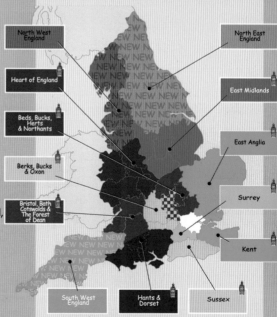

Farms, Wildlife & Nature Parks

Flora and fauna at its best for you to enjoy.

BRISTOL & BATH AREA

Banwell, Court Farm Country Park, Wolvershill Road, 01934 822383. Help bottle feed the baby animals, take a Big Cat ride or in Summer tackle the Maize Maze. Outdoor play area and huge indoor play barns. Open Summer, daily, 10am-5.30pm, Winter, closed Mons. Schools Birthdays **Winter Price B.**

Bath, Prior Park Landscape Garden, NT, Ralph Allen Drive, www.nationaltrust.org.uk 01225 833422 (24hr Information Line, 09001 335242). This lovely garden has a Palladian bridge, fish ponds and fine views. No car park but reduced admission for those arriving by public transport. Sturdy shoes recommended. Family events. Open Feb-Nov, Wed-Mon, 11am-5.30pm (or dusk if earlier; Dec-Jan, Fri-Sun. Schools **Winter Price B.**

Bath (near), Norwood Farm, Norton St Philip, 01373 834356, is a working organic farm with native rare breeds of cattle, goats and sheep. A lovely opportunity to see lambing in Spring. Play areas. Open 23rd Mar-late Sept, daily, 10.30am-5.30pm. Schools Birthdays **Price B.**

Bristol, Bristol Zoo Gardens, Clifton, www.bristolzoo.org.uk 0117 974 7300. Visit 'Zona Brazil', the new Brazilian exhibit at Bristol Zoo Gardens and other favourites including 'Seal & Penguin Coasts' with fantastic underwater viewing, Bug World, Twilight World, the Monkey House, the Reptile House, and the children's play area. The popular Activity Centre, the Zoolympics trail, special events and feeding time talks make it an educational as well as enjoyable day out. There is so much to experience at Bristol Zoo Gardens, with over 300 species of wildlife in beautiful gardens, your day will certainly be packed full of fun, facts and fantastic animals. Open daily, 9am-approx 5.30pm (4.30pm in Winter). Schools Birthdays **Winter Price C Check out page 39.**

Wildwalk@Bristol, Anchor Road, Harbourside, www.at-bristol.org.uk 0845 3451235. An eye-opening exhibition of the natural world, from a coral reef to a tropical forest, from fossils to conservation and from amazing plants to thousands of tiny live creatures. Part of the At-Bristol Complex, check out `Historic Sites'. Open daily, 10am-6pm. Schools Birthdays **Winter Price B.**

Bristol (near), HorseWorld - Visitors Centre, Staunton Manor Farm, Staunton Lane, Whitchurch, off the A37, www.horseworld.org.uk 01275 540173. A registered equine welfare charity offering a great family day out. Meet over 40 of the 300 rescued horses, ponies and donkeys. From Shetland ponies to shire horses, each has a different story to tell. Other attractions at HorseWorld include interactive museums, a video film presentation, pony rides, pony and pet handling, indoor and outdoor play areas, a nature trail, picnic areas, restaurant and gift shop. Open until 28th Sept, daily, 10am-4pm (5pm from 22nd Mar); from 29th Sept, Tues-Sun, 10am-4pm, and daily in school hols. Closed 22nd Dec-1st Jan. Schools Birthdays **Winter Price B.**

Keynsham, Avon Valley Country Park, www.avonvalleycountrypark.co.uk 0117 9864929, covers 32 acres with animals, play areas, assault course, mini quad bikes, boating and mini steam train rides. Open end Mar-Oct, Tues-Sun, Bank Hol Mons & daily in school hols, 10am-6pm. Schools Birthdays **Price B.**

Steep Holm Island, is owned and run by a charity, the Kenneth Allsop Trust, as a wildlife sanctuary. From Apr-Oct boat trips can be made to the island which lies about 5 miles offshore of Weston-super-Mare. Check out 'Trips'. **Price E.**

Birdland
- Park & Gardens -

A day out in Bourton-on-the-Water must include a visit to BIRDLAND.
Set in seven acres of woodland, gardens, rivers and ponds, BIRDLAND is home to over 500 birds from around the world.

Open All Year from 10am - 6pm
(last admission 1 hour before closing)

For further information of admission and winter times please phone

01451 820480

RISSINGTON ROAD · BOURTON-ON-THE-WATER · GLOUCESTERSHIRE

Keep a sharp eye open for our Special

BIRD OF PREY
ENCOUNTER DAYS

Choose a day to come and visit
Hawks & Owls at close quarters!
These days will be running throughout the Summer.
Ring for more information.

Thornbury (near), Oldown Country Park, Tockington, www.oldown.co.uk 01454 413605. Tackle the Forest Challenge or visit the woodland play area. Then there are animals, pedal go-karts and miniature train rides. Open Feb half term-Oct half term: Sat-Sun, 10am-5pm; Jun-Jul, Tues-Sun; daily in school hols. Schools Birthdays **Price B.**

Weston-super-Mare, SeaQuarium, Marine Parade, www.seaquarium.co.uk 01934 641603. A dramatic underwater tunnel, variety of environments, touchpools and the `Lethal Reef Zone' guarantee a visit here is full of interest for all ages. Open Summer, daily, 10am-5pm. Telephone for Winter opening. Schools **Winter Price B.**

Wraxall, Noah's Ark Zoo Farm, Failand Road, 6 miles W of Bristol, www.noahsarkfarmcentre.co.uk 01275 852606, is home to over 50 species of animals and birds. Hold tiny chicks and visit exhibitions and huge play areas. Open from 22nd Feb, telephone for details. Schools Birthdays **Price B.**

GLOUCESTERSHIRE

Berkeley, Butterfly Farm, Berkeley Castle, 01453 511209. Admire the tropical butterflies fluttering around you. Open 1st Apr-end Sept, Wed-Sat & Bank Hol Mons, 12noon-4pm, Sun, 2-5pm. Schools **Price A.**

Berkeley (near), Cattle Country Adventure Park, www.cattlecountry.co.uk 01453 810510, has a herd of American bison and other animals. There are extensive indoor and outdoor play areas (try the Zip Wire!) and a Willow Maze. Open Suns, 10am-5pm; closed late Dec. Also open, Easter-end Aug, Sats; Easter & Summer school hols, daily; and for private bookings. Schools Birthdays **Winter Price B/C.**

Bibury, Bibury Trout Farm, 01285 740215. The waters come to life as you feed the fish! Learn about Rainbow Trout and visit the Catch Your Own fishery (check opening). A play area is planned for 2003. Open Summer, Mon-Sat, 9am-6pm, Sun, 10am-6pm (5pm Winter). Schools **Winter Price A.**

Bourton-on-the-Water, Birdland, Rissington Road, 01451 820480, is home to over 500 birds in a natural setting of woodland, river and gardens. Flamingos, pelicans, penguins and storks can be seen in water habitats and parrots, hornbills, toucans and many more birds are housed in the aviaries. The more delicate species can be found in the Tropical and Desert Houses. Look out for Penguin Feeding Time which is a particular favourite with children! Bird of Prey Encounter Days are held during the Summer and there is now a Bird Adoption scheme in operation. Call in at the information centre to learn more about birds and to keep up to date with the latest news. Open daily, Apr-Oct,10am-6pm, Nov-Mar,10am-4pm. Schools **Winter Price B** Check out page 36.

Cirencester (near), The Butts Farm, South Cerney, 01285 862205. A family-run farm. Feed and cuddle the animals, ride a pony or take a tractor safari. Collect stickers with each activity. Play area. Open Apr-Oct, Wed-Sun, 11am-5pm, & daily in school hols; also for Spring lambing. Schools Birthdays **Price B.**

Coleford (near), Puzzle Wood, on B4228 Chepstow Road, 01594 833187. The deep ravines, wooden bridges and moss covered rocks of this maze create a magical landscape. Baby carriers needed! Indoor Wood Puzzle and farm animals. Open Easter-Oct, Tues-Sun & Bank Hol Mons, 11am-5.30pm (4pm Oct). Schools **Price B.**

Cranham, Prinknash Abbey Bird and Deer Park, www.prinknash-bird-and-deerpark.com 01452 812727. Hand-feed peacocks, waterfowl and fallow deer in this small park or throw food to the trout before visiting the Tudor Wendy house. Open daily, 10am-5pm (4pm Winter). Closed Good Fri. Schools **Winter Price B.**

Gloucester, Barn Owl Centre, The Tithe Barn, Brockworth Court, www.barnowl.co.uk 01452 865999. This small, friendly centre cares for captive bred birds of prey, many rescued from cruelty. Flying displays by appointment. Open Mon-Sat & Bank Hols, 10am-5pm, Sun, 12noon-5pm. Schools Birthdays **Winter Price A.**

Guiting Power, Cotswold Farm Park, www.cotswoldfarmpark.co.uk 01451 850307, specialises in rare breeds. There are seasonal demonstrations, a Touch Barn, Pets Corner, exciting adventure playground and Tractor Driving School. Open: 29th Mar-14th Sept, daily, 10.30am-5pm; 14th Sept-end Oct, Sat-Sun (daily, Autumn half term), 10.30am-4pm. Schools Birthdays **Price B.**

Longhope, Mohair Countryside Centre, Little London, 8 miles W of Gloucester, off A40, www.mohaircentre.net 01452 831137. Meet Grunty the Pig and friends in the Pets Corner, explore 100 acres of countryside and then visit the playzones. Outside there is a giant sandpit, water spot, pedal zone, adventure play corner and adjacent picnic area. The indoor area covers approximately 800 square metres and includes play equipment with slides and ball pools. Farm and Rural information and a Toy Corner, plus gift shop and restaurant. The facilities are most suitable for toddlers to ten year olds. Open daily, 10.30am-5pm. Closed Mon-Tues in term time. Schools Birthdays **Winter Price B Check out page 48.**

Moreton-in-Marsh, Cotswold Falconry Centre, Batsford Park, www.cotswold-falconry.co.uk 01386 701043, has four flying displays daily, featuring eagles, hawks, falcons and owls. Use CCTV to watch the nests in the breeding aviaries. Open mid Feb-mid Nov, daily, 10.30am-5.30pm. Schools Birthdays **Price B.**

Newent (near), National Birds of Prey Centre, www.nbpc.co.uk 0870 9901992. See over 80 species of birds of prey ranging from huge eagles to tiny owls. Flying demonstrations are held three times a day. Open Feb-Oct, daily, 10.30am-5.30pm (or dusk if earlier); also for Winter Owl Evenings. Schools Birthdays **Price B.**

Painswick, Painswick Rococo Garden, www.rococogarden.co.uk 01452 813204. This six-acre garden has a young yew maze, nature trail and striking architecture to intrigue children. Try and see the snowdrops in February. Open mid Jan-end Oct, daily, 11am-5pm. Schools **Price A.**

Slimbridge, Wildfowl and Wetlands Trust, www.wwt.org.uk 01453 890333, is an award-winning 800 acre reserve and home to the world's largest collection of exotic (and greedy!) wildfowl. Visitor Centre with `hands on' displays and special events during school hols. Open daily, 9.30am-5pm (4pm Winter). Schools Birthdays **Winter Price B.**

Tetbury (near), Westonbirt, The National Arboretum, www.forestry.gov.uk/westonbirt 01666 880220. Explore 600 acres of trees, ranging from giant Redwoods to delicate acacias. Discovery days for children. Open daily, 10am-8pm (or dusk if earlier); 'The Enchanted Wood', mid Nov-mid Dec, Fri-Sun, 5-7pm. Schools **Winter Price B.**

WILTSHIRE

Calne (near), Bowood House and Gardens, www.bowood.org 01249 812102. One of the most beautiful parks in the country, landscaped by 'Capability' Brown with sloping lawns stretching away from the House to the lake beyond. This 100 acre park contains many exotic trees in the arboretum and pinetum, a Cascade Waterfall, Doric Temple and Hermit's Cave. For children of 12 and under, Bowood offers a truly outstanding adventure playground, complete with life size pirate ship, giant slides, chutes and high level rope walks and the famous Space Dive. There is also an indoor soft play palace for under 8s. Open daily, 1st Apr-2nd Nov, 11am-6pm or dusk if earlier. Birthdays **Price B Check out 'Historic Sites' and page 33.**

Cholderton, Cholderton Rare Breeds Farm Park, just off A303 between Amesbury and Andover, www.rabbitworld.co.uk 01980 629438. Discover a wonderful variety of attractions. Children are encouraged to touch and feed the animals or even take one for a walk. Visit Rabbit World to see over 50 different breeds or explore the replica Iron Age Farm. There are archaeology days for children and a dig in August. Don't miss the hilarious 'Pork Stakes' Pig Races! Indoor and outdoor play and picnic areas, pony rides, nature trail, shop and tea-room. Telephone for opening times. Schools Birthdays **Winter Price B Check out below.**

Highworth (near), Roves Farm, Sevenhampton, www.rovesfarm.co.uk 01793 763939. Fun, whatever the weather. Animals to meet and feed, Spring lambing, nature trails, indoor and outdoor adventure play and a Willow Maze. Open mid Mar-end Oct half term, Wed-Sun, 10.30am-5pm, daily in school hols. Schools Birthdays **Price B.**

Lacock, Lackham Country Park, www.lackham.co.uk 01249 466800. Gardens with a children's laurel maze, a Museum, animal park, woodland trails and special events provide plenty of interest. Open May-Aug, Sun & Bank Hol Mons, 10am-5pm; also Aug, Tues-Thurs and at other times for groups. Schools **Price A.**

Teffont, Farmer Giles Farmstead, www.farmergiles.co.uk 01722 716338. Watch the cows being milked and bottle or hand feed different animals on this working farm. Indoor and outdoor play areas. Open Mar-mid Sept, daily, 10am-6pm, Winter, Sat-Sun & daily in school hols. Schools Birthdays **Winter Price B.**

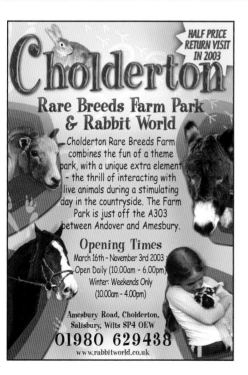
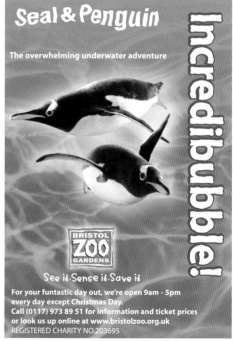

Tollard Royal, Larmer Tree Gardens, Rushmore Estate, www.larmertreegardens.co.uk 01725 516228. The grounds here have ornamental birds, an adventure playground and an exhibition of colonial and oriental buildings with children's trail. Open Apr-Jun & Aug-Oct, Sun-Fri, 11am-6pm. **Price B.**

Warminster, Longleat Safari Park, off A36, on A362 Warminster to Frome road, www.longleat.co.uk 01985 844400. Voted 'UK Family Attraction of the Year 2002' by 'The Good Britain Guide', Longleat is a great day out for all the family. Discover lions, tigers, elephants and giraffe within this world famous Safari Park before going on to explore the many attractions combined within the Longleat Passport: Longleat House, the World's Longest Hedge Maze, Safari Boats, the Adventure Castle and the Blue Peter Maze, Longleat Railway, Pets Corner, Postman Pat Village and more. A Passport includes one visit to all 12 attractions with the option of returning before the end of the season (2nd Nov 2003) to complete any attractions not previously visited. All attractions open daily, 5th Apr-2nd Nov. Schools Birthdays **Price G Check out 'Historic Sites' chapter and page 33.**

West Knoyle, Bush Farm Bison Centre, www.bisonfarm.co.uk 01747 830263. Herds of red deer, elk and bison make this a farm walk with a difference. In the farmyard are chipmunks and traditional English livestock. Open Apr-Sept, Wed-Sun, 10am-5pm. Schools **Price B.**

Westbury (near), Brokerswood Country Park, www.brokerswoodcountrypark.com 01373 822238, is 80 acres of woodland with trails, two adventure playgrounds, a narrow gauge railway (check operating times), undercover play areas and Heritage Centre. Open daily, 10am-5pm. Schools Birthdays **Winter Price A.**

Boat, Bus & Train Trips

It is exciting to be going somewhere and today, when so many of us travel by car, it becomes a real adventure for children to experience some other forms of transport. Do your children go for bus rides very often? Have you ever thought of going on a river trip or a coastal cruise? Why not step back in time and enjoy a steam train ride? There are many opportunities listed below to try out different forms of transport. A journey in itself is good fun, let alone the destination, but a combination of both gives the ingredients for a successful and enjoyable day out.

BOAT TRIPS

BRISTOL AND BATH AREA

Bath, Pulteney Bridge, 01225 466407. **The Bath Boating Station,** a unique boating facility, offers motorised trips for those wishing to receive a conducted tour of the river. Punts, canoes and skiffs are available for hire from Forester Road, Bathwick. Open Apr-Sept, daily, 10am-6pm. Telephone for Winter opening times. Schools **Price B Check out 'Directory of Activities' and page 43.**
Pulteney Weir, 01225 460831. A return trip up the River Avon on this 10-seater takes 1^1/$_2$ hours. Commentary on the wildlife available. Operates Mar-Nov, daily. Schools **Price A.**
Riverside/Pulteney Weir, 07980 335185. One hour return trips on the River Avon with commentary, Mar-Nov, daily. Schools **Price B.**

Bristol, City Docks, www.bristolferryboat.co.uk 0117 9273416. Daily 'round trip' and 'waterbus' services on the historic harbour. Stops include SS Great Britain and At-Bristol. Also charter trips. Schools **Winter.**
Cumberland Basin, www.waverleyexcursions.co.uk 0845 1304647. Sail to Clevedon (short one way cruise), Ilfracombe, Wales or along the Somerset coast in Summer. Schools Birthdays.
Floating Harbour, www.bristolpacket.co.uk 0117 9268157. Tours of the city docks with commentary operate Sat-Sun & daily in school hols. Also available, cruises between Avonmouth and Bath and charter trips. Schools **Winter.**
Floating Harbour, 0117 9293659. Hour long trips with commentary and ferry boat service (40 minute round trip) at weekends & daily in school hols. Schools **Winter.**
Industrial Museum. Occasional trips on historic steam tug from outside the museum. Check out 'Free Places'. **Price A.**

Clevedon, The Pier, www.waverleyexcursions.co.uk 0845 1304647. Summer cruises to Bristol, the Welsh, Somerset and Devon coasts, Sharpness, the Holm Islands, Lundy and on the River Severn. Also, occasional cruises from Portishead and Weston-super-Mare. Schools Birthdays.

Monkton Combe, Brassknocker Basin, www.bath-narrowboat-trips.co.uk 01373 813957. Public and charter trips along the Kennet and Avon canal from Easter-Oct. Schools **Price B.**

Weston-super-Mare, Knightstone Causeway, 01934 632307. Day trips run to Steep Holm Island nature reserve from Apr-Oct. Check out 'Farms'. **Price E.**

GLOUCESTERSHIRE

Cirencester (near), Coates, www.cotswoldcanals.com 07929 980670. Sapperton Canal Tunnel Boat Trips run (water level permitting) on Suns in Winter and for groups by arrangement. Most suitable for 7 years and over. Schools **Price A.**

Gloucester, Merchants Quay, www.nwm.org.uk 01452 318200. A forty-five minute return canal trip; longer trips available. Check out National Waterways Museum in 'Historic Sites' and telephone for times. Schools Birthdays **Price B.**

Lechlade, **Halfpenny Bridge,** www.rivercruises.co.uk 01793 574499. Planning to start in 2003, public and charter trips on the River Thames, Apr-Sept. Schools **Price A.**

Riverside Park, www.costwoldcanals.com 01446 760314. Half-hour return trips on the river Thames operate from early Summer. Longer trips are planned. Schools Birthdays **Price A.**

Sharpness, **Old Dock,** www.waverleyexcursions.co.uk 0845 1304647. Occasional Summer cruises to Clevedon and the Devon coast. Return by coach. Schools Birthdays.

Stonehouse(near), **Eastington,** www.cotswoldcanals.com 01453 545042. Take a trip on the Stroudwater Navigation passing through Blunder Lock. Operates Easter-Sept and for 'Santa Cruises' in Dec. Schools **Price A.**

Tewkesbury, **Mill Street or Riverside Walk,** www.telstarcruisers.co.uk 01684 294088. A ferry service on the River Avon connects Tewkesbury, Twyning and Bredon, Easter-end Sept. Charter trips also available. Schools.

WILTSHIRE

Bradford-on-Avon, Upper Wharf, www.katrust.org 01225 868683. Public and charter trips, Easter-Oct, along the Kennet & Avon Canal. Schools **Price B.**

Devizes, The Wharf, www.whitehorseboats.co.uk 01380 728504. Trips on locally built narrow boats along the Kennet & Avon Canal from Easter-Sept. Schools **Price B.**

BUS TRIPS

BRISTOL AND BATH AREA

Tickets for these open top bus trips are valid all day giving the chance to stay on board for the full tour and also use the bus as a taxi service later, hopping on and off at any of the stops.

Bath, High Street/Grand Parade, 01225 330444. Trips of about $1/2$ hour with audio tour run daily Apr-Oct and on weekends in Winter. Schools **Winter Price B.**
Terrace Walk, 07721 559686. A trip with live commentary takes about $1/2$ hour. Operates daily, but check in Winter. Schools **Winter Price B.**

Bristol, Tourist Information Centre, www.bristolvisitor.co.uk 0117 9260767 (Information Centre). From Apr-Sept, hour-long tours run each day with live commentary. Schools **Price B.**

TRAIN TRIPS

BRISTOL AND BATH AREA

Bitton, Avon Valley Railway, www.avonvalleyrailway.co.uk 0117 9327296 (24 hour talking timetable) or 0117 9325538 (general enquiries). Conveniently situated midway between Bristol and Bath, the Avon Valley Railway is an enjoyable day out for children and adults alike. Take a forty-five minute journey on a steam train, enjoy the beautiful scenery and then admire the restored engines. There are many special events for children, including a 'Day out with Thomas' in May and Oct, and Santa Specials. Group bookings welcome. Station and buffet open daily, 10.30am-5pm. Steam trains operate Suns & Bank Hols from Easter to Oct; also Weds and Thurs in Aug, and for Christmas specials. Prices vary. Schools Birthdays **Check out page 43.**

Bristol, Industrial Museum. Take a short trip on a steam train along the docks from the museum. Check out 'Free Places'. **Price A.**

Weston-super-Mare, Weston Miniature Railway, Marine Parade, 01934 643510. Miniature NG locomotives run for just over half a mile around the putting course and along the Beach Lawns. Open Spring Bank Hol-mid Sept, daily, from 10.30am, weather permitting. **Price A.**

GLOUCESTERSHIRE

Coleford (near), **Perrygrove Railway,** on the B4228, www.perrygrove.co.uk 01594 834991. Trips on the 15" NG steam railway, a treasure hunt and the indoor village with its secret passages. Telephone for operating days. Schools Birthdays **Price B.**

Lydney, **Dean Forest Railway,** Norchard Railway Centre, Forest Road, www.deanforestrailway.co.uk 01594 845840 or 843423 (24hr). Nostalgic trips by steam train or, occasionally, by diesel heritage MU. Look out for special events. Open daily for static display. Trains operate Mar-Oct and Santa specials in Dec. Schools Birthdays.

Toddington, **Gloucestershire Warwickshire Railway,** www.gwsr.plc.uk 01242 621405. The grand opening of Cheltenham Racecourse Station takes place on 12th April 2003. Thereafter a round trip along part of the former Great Western main line will cover 20 miles. Special events for children include a 'Day out with Thomas' on 5th-6th April and 9th-10th August, an Emergency Services day and Model Railway Exhibition. Catch a 'Santa Special' in December (advance booking essential). A narrow gauge steam railway runs alongside the main car park on selected weekends and there is an exhibition, gift shop and tearoom. Also board at Winchcombe and Cheltenham Racecourse. Operates most weekends & daily in some school hols. Schools Birthdays **Winter Check out page 44.**

WILTSHIRE

Swindon (near), **Swindon & Cricklade Railway,** Blunsdon Station, between Swindon and Cricklade, off A419, www.swindon-cricklade-railway.org 01793 771615. Trips by steam on special events days and by diesel at other times. Restoration centre and old signal box. Trains operate, Suns, Bank Hol Mons & at other times for special events. Site also open Sats. Schools Birthdays **Winter.**

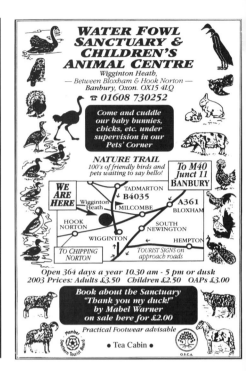

44

Places to go outside the area

Visit some exciting places just a little further afield.

BERKSHIRE

Windsor, Legoland,® www.legoland.co.uk 08705 040404. Imagine an exciting land of adventure and fun for children where the entertainment is definitely `hands on'. Ride the thrilling Dragon Coaster into the castle dungeons or drive a LEGOLAND® car. You can even brave the Pirate Falls log flume and explore the world famous Miniland, made from over 35 million Lego® bricks. In the LEGO Creation Centre, spot the famous faces in the LEGOLAND Hall of Fame and wonder at the Crown Jewels made entirely of LEGO bricks. For high speed thrills and spills, catch the action-packed Racers 4D movie in the Imagination Theatre. With over 40 interactive rides, playscapes, workshops, shows and attractions set in 150 acres of beautiful parkland, LEGOLAND Windsor offers a full and exciting day for children aged 2-12 and their families. School/group bookings telephone 01753 626800. Open 28th Mar-2nd Nov from 10am (closing times vary). Schools Birthdays **Price G Check out page 46.**

LONDON

Chelsea, National Army Museum, Royal Hospital Road, www.national-army-museum.ac.uk 020 7730 0717. The colourful story of the British Army, from Agincourt to the present day. Find out the facts behind some of the remarkable episodes in Britain's history and the experiences of the men and women involved. Try out kit from different eras, survey a huge model of Waterloo, explore a reproduction First World War trench and test modern military skills in exciting computer challenges. Discover portraits by Reynolds and Gainsborough, a lamp used by Florence Nightingale, and even the skeleton of Napoleon's horse! The ordinary soldier's story is brought vividly to life. Regular weekend special events. Entrance is free to this museum. Open daily, 10am-5.30pm. Schools Winter **Price F.**

OXFORDSHIRE

Burford, Cotswold Wildlife Park, www.cotswoldwildlifepark.co.uk 01993 823006, occupies 160 acres of gardens and parkland with a wide variety of animals to be seen. The wildlife varies from reptiles to tarantulas, penguins to rhinos as well as endangered Asiatic lions, Amur leopards and Red Pandas in large enclosures. Children will love to watch the antics of the lively gibbons and meerkats. Extensive shaded picnic lawns also provide the setting for a large adventure playground. A brass-rubbing centre and cafeteria are located in a listed Victorian Manor. Special events throughout the Summer and a narrow-gauge railway runs from Apr-Oct. The Park encourages school parties. Open daily at 10am. Please check for closing times. Schools **Winter Price C Check out page 44.**

Wigginton Heath, The Water Fowl Sanctuary and Children's Animal Centre, off the A361 Banbury to Chipping Norton road, www.visitbritain.com 01608 730252. Come and talk to the animals at this friendly, family-run, countryside haven! Whatever the time of year there are always baby animals for children to handle, with a little help from the adults. Visit the ponies, donkey and pigs or feed the rare breeds of poultry. See some ancient breeds of sheep, goats and cattle. There are aviary birds, geese, rheas, even an ostrich and an emu and lots of different species of ducks. Let off steam in the children's play area, there is plenty of space to picnic too in this rural and informal setting. Practical clothing and wellies are a good idea in wet weather. Reduced rates are available for pre-booked groups of 10 or more. Open daily, 10.30am-5pm, or dusk in winter. **Winter Price B Check out page 44.**

THREE BRILLIANT EXCUSES TO GO TO THE AMAZEMENT PARK

The Adventurer's Express will take you on a train safari around the LEGOLAND Park. LEGO Racers 4D is a unique visual experience that literally puts you in the driving seat. Brave the Dragon coaster as it travels through the heights and depths of the Castle, past animated LEGO models: there are jugglers, jesters, cooks and magicians - conjuring up interesting spells.

With over 50 interactive rides, live shows, building workshops driving schools and attractions, all set in 150 acres of beautiful Parkland, LEGOLAND is more than a day out, it's a life time of memories.

Start planning your day out at the amazement park today. Phone 08705 04 04 04 or visit www.legoland.co.uk

08705 04 04 04   www.legoland.co.uk

LEGOLAND WINDSOR

SOMERSET

Cranmore, East Somerset Railway, off the A361 Frome to Shepton Mallet, www.eastsomersetrailway.org 01749 880417. Discover a bygone age on a trip by steam train through the beautiful Somerset countryside. Special events are held throughout the year. 'Thomas the Tank Engine' and 'Sir Topham Hatt, the Fat Controller', will be visiting at Easter and from 16th-17th August. 'Santa Specials' run in December with a present and seasonal refreshments included (advance booking required and one ride only). Unlimited rides on 'Thomas' days and normal service days. Trains operate & restaurant open most weekends throughout the year; also Weds in Jun & Jul, and Weds & Thurs in Aug. Shop, Art Gallery & Sheds are open daily. Schools Birthdays Winter Price B Check out page 44.

SUSSEX

Cambridge Language & Activity Courses. CLAC, www.clac.org.uk 01223 240340, organises interesting Summer courses for 8-13 year and 14-17 year olds at two separate sites in lovely countryside locations, Lavant House and Slindon College, West Sussex. The idea is to bring together British and foreign students to create natural language exchange in a motivated and fun environment. There are French, German and Spanish classes for British students and English for overseas students. Fully supervised in a safe environment, there are lots of activities such as swimming, tennis, team games and competitions, drama and music, in addition to the language tuition. Residential or not, these courses offer enjoyable multi-activity weeks with 20 hours of specific tuition in small groups. Courses run weekly during July and August. Please call for more details and a brochure. Birthdays Check out below.

'Let's Go with the Children' guides now cover all counties in England. Collect the set. Check out page 34.

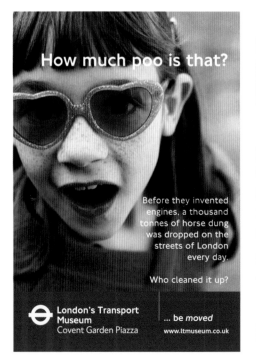
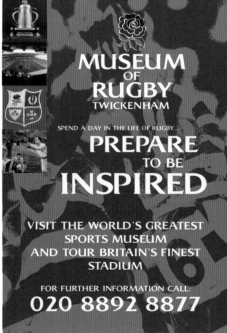

London

LET'S VISIT LONDON

BBC Television Centre Tours, Wood Lane, Shepherd's Bush, www.bbc.co.uk/tours 0870 6030304. Take a tour of BBC Television Centre in Shepherd's Bush and see what happens within the most famous TV Centre in the world. Thousands of programmes are produced here every year including favourites such as Top of the Pops, Blue Peter, Parkinson, CBBC and more. On your tour you are likely to see into studios, visit BBC News, enter into the Top of the Pops Star Bar, have a play within the interactive studio and much more. Tours run 6 times a day, Mon-Sat and last for up to two hours. Tours are available for anyone over the age of 10 yrs and must be pre-booked. Television Centre is a working building so studio activity on the day of your visit cannot be guaranteed. The nearest Tube Station is White City on the Central Line. A Public Car Park is available 2 minutes walk away down Ariel Way. Schools **Winter Price C.**

London's Transport Museum, Covent Garden Piazza, www.ltmuseum.co.uk 020 7565 7299 (recorded information), 020 7379 6344 (education service), using imaginative and dynamic displays, takes you on a fascinating journey through time and recounts the story of the interaction between transport, the capital and its people from 1800 to the present day. Look out for the under 5s funbus, try the bus and tube simulators, meet characters from the past, see models and working displays and get interactive in the many 'KidZones'. More fun learning than you would have thought possible! Good educational material and lots of special holiday activities. There is now free admission for children under 16. Open daily, 10am-6pm, but 11am-6pm on Fridays. Schools **Winter Price B Check out page 48.**

National Army Museum, Royal Hospital Road, Chelsea. **Please see entry on page 45.**

Museum of Rugby and Twickenham Stadium Tour, Rugby Road, Twickenham www.rfu.com 020 8892 8877. Prepare to be inspired spending a day in the life of rugby! From the moment you pass through the authentic Twickenham turnstile, you'll be immersed in a world of Rugby history. Enjoy some of the finest and most extensive collection of rugby memorabilia in the world. Let interactive touch-screen computers, video footage and period set pieces take you on a journey through the history of the game. Also operating from the Museum are tours of the rugby stadium. Expert tour guides will take you on an awe-inspiring journey through the home of England rugby. Walk alongside the hallowed turf, visit England's dressing room and experience the excitement of match day as you enter the stadium through the players' tunnel. Open daily, Tues-Sat & Bank Hols 10am-5pm, Sun 11-5pm. Match days are open to match ticket holders only. Closed Good Fri. Schools **Winter** Birthdays **Price B Check out page 48.**

Shakespeare's Globe, New Globe Walk, Bankside, www.shakespeares-globe.org, 0207 9021515 (exhibition and tour). 0207 401 9919 (box office), 0207 902 1433 (education), is a faithful reconstruction of the playhouse in which Shakespeare worked and for which he wrote many of his most memorable plays. Performances in the theatre take place between May and Sept. You can take a guided tour of today's working theatre or visit Shakespeare's Globe Exhibition which provides a unique year-round introduction to the theatre and London of Shakespeare's time. In the vast UnderGlobe beneath the theatre, every aspect of Shakespeare's work is brought imaginatively to life using a combination of modern technology and traditional crafts. The roles of actor, musician and audience are explored against a backdrop of Elizabethan Bankside, the Soho of Shakespeare's day! Open daily for exhibition and tours 10am-5pm. Schools **Winter Price C. Check out page 50.**

Somerset House, Strand, www.somerset-house.org.uk 020 7420 9406 (Education Department). After extensive renovation, this magnificent building is now open to the public for the first time as a place for enjoyment, fun and refreshments as well as arts and culture. Somerset House is the inspirational setting for the world famous art collection of the Courtauld Institute, the

gold, silver and decorative arts of the Gilbert Collection, and the Hermitage Rooms, which provide London with a unique window on Russian art and history. The courtyard with its beautiful fountains is at the centre of Somerset House, providing a wonderful setting for family fun, especially on summer days. A full range of school and family activities is on offer throughout the year. Open daily 10am-6pm. For more information please call or email education@somerset-house.org.uk Schools **Winter Price A** (per adult per collection) Under 18s free. **Check out page 50.**

LET'S TAKE A TRIP

London Frogtours, on the South Bank at Westminster Bridge behind County Hall, www.frogtours.com 0207 928 3132, offer a unique 70-minute amazing adventure tour of London's famous sights by road and river on board an amphibious frog! Voted 'London Family Attraction of the Year' by the Good Britain Guide 2002, the tour takes in many points of interest between the Houses of Parliament, Downing Street, Buckingham Palace, Piccadilly and Westminster Abbey before a dramatic launch into the Thames for the water borne part of the tour! Tours run daily, duration may vary due to road and river conditions. **Winter Price E Check out page 54.**

On the River Thames with City Cruises, www.citycruises.com 02077 400 400. Add some excitement for the children, a new perspective for everyone and get excellent value by seeing some of London's best sights from the River Thames aboard a City Cruises luxury river-liner using a brand new River Red Rover ticket! You can also now travel as far as Greenwich to see the Cutty Sark. For just £8.50 for an adult ticket, £4.25 for a child or just £21 for a family ticket, you can use a hop-on hop-off service between the major destination piers on the River! From Westminster Pier services run every 20 minutes to Tower Pier, and, every 40 minutes to Greenwich via Waterloo and Tower Pier. Your River Red Rover will give you unlimited daily travel between these piers. Admire the Houses of Parliament and Big Ben, see St Paul's Cathedral, look out for the Tate Modern, see if you can spot Shakespeare's Globe. Lots to see from these super boats with cafe style facilities and a capacity of 520 seats which operate every day of the year. **Winter Price C Check out page 52.**

Canal Waterbus, 020 7482 2660(information), 020 7482 2550(bookings), will enable you to see a side of London that you never knew existed. Take a boat trip along the Regents Canal, through the green and leafy Regents Park and the dark mysterious Maida Hill Tunnel. Boats leave from Camden Lock, with its unique atmosphere and unusual shopping, and/or Little Venice, with its island, ducks and boats. You can stop off at London Zoo to visit the animals via a special canal gate. Excellent educational resources and special group rates. Trips run daily Apr-Oct, weekends only Nov-Mar. Schools **Winter PriceB/E.**

The Original Tour, London Sightseeing Bus Tours, www.theoriginaltour.com 020 8877 2120. An open top bus ride is a wonderful way to travel and introduce children to the splendid sights of London. The Original Tour offers an excellent service, with over 90 stops to hop-on and off, an entertaining commentary available on board all of the buses, and their famous 'Kids Club'. Children are both entertained and educated by the special commentary designed for them, as magical stories about London unfold with tales from Roman times until the present day. Listen out for the ghostly 'Spirit of London'. The service runs frequently, seven days a week, from a variety of easily accessed stops. Times vary seasonally for each route. To celebrate over 50 years of sightseeing The Original Tour are now giving every customer a free Thames River Cruise! For more information or to enjoy a special discount call 020 8877 2120 or visit www.theoriginaltour.com and quote LGWC. **Winter Price G Check out page 54.**

LET'S PLAY

Snakes and Ladders, Syon Park, Brentford, snakes-and-ladders.co.uk 020 8847 0946, is well signposted from Syon Park or can be accessed via 237 or 267 bus from Kew Bridge BR or Gunnersbury Underground Station. Children can find action packed fun whatever the weather. They can let off steam in the giant supervised indoor main playframe, intermediate 2-5s area or

toddlers area or use the outdoor adventure playground when the sun shines. A mini motor bike circuit provides an exciting additional activity. Meanwhile parents can relax in the cafe overlooking the playframe. Open daily 10am-6pm. Last admission 5.15pm. All children must wear socks. Schools Birthdays **Winter.**

LET'S GO TO A CAFE

The Clay Café, 8-10 Monkville Parade, Finchley Road, Temple Fortune, www.theclaycafe.co.uk 020 8905 5353, is a hub of cuisine and entertainment that positively welcomes families with children of all ages. This intriguing combination of a full service bistro style restaurant plus a paint-it-yourself ceramic studio offers a fresh and innovative approach to providing creative relaxation for both adults and children alike. Choose from over 200 pieces of pottery (dinnerware, vases, animals etc) and a qualified Art Technician will assist you in creating a unique masterpiece! Glass painting and T-shirt painting are also on offer. Open Sun-Fri 11am-10pm, Sat 10am-11pm. Schools Birthdays **Winter Prices vary.**

LET'S GO TO THE THEATRE

Les Miserables, Palace Theatre, suitable for 8-18+ year olds, is a tale of passion and destruction set in the period of the French Revolution. Educational resource packs are available free of charge and backstage tours can be booked in conjunction with school visits to the performance, 020 7439 3062. Schools **Winter Price on application.**

The Miz Kids Club, at the Palace Theatre, 020 7439 3062, is based on the legendary production of Les Miserables. The club consists of a backstage tour of the Palace Theatre, a snack lunch, a drama and singing workshop, the opportunity to meet a member of the cast, and an exclusive certificate of attendance! This is a great introduction to the themes and characters in this internationally acclaimed musical by Boublil and Schonberg. Clubs run on Saturday mornings, 10.45am-1.30pm, twice monthly, for two age groups: 8-11 years and 12-15 years. Packages, including tickets for the matinee performance and The Miz Kids Club, start at £23. The club alone is £15 if you cannot make the performance on the same day. Early booking is recommended. Call John Scarborough or Julia Dyal. **Winter Check out page 54.**

The Lion King, Lyceum Theatre, Wellington Street, www.disney.co.uk/MusicalTheatre 0870 243 9000 (ticket hotline), 020 7845 0949 (group bookings). One of the most successful Disney films in history, stunningly recreated on stage, is a thrilling and original musical which brings a rich sense of Africa to the stage through a medley of exotic sights and sounds. The show opens in the well loved Disney setting of 'Pride Rock' where 'Simba' the new lion cub is presented to a magical parade of Safari animals. One cannot fail to appreciate the inspiration that allows the giraffes to strut, the birds to swoop and the gazelles to bound. This initial spectacle is breathtaking as the entire savannah comes to life. Wonder at the creativity of the set as the sun rises, savannah plains sway, cattle stampede, drought takes hold and starry skies give up their secrets. Huge variety is offered in the musical score ranging from pulsating African rhythms to contemporary rock. Tim Rice and Elton John's Oscar winning work is unforgettable. A show not to be missed. **Winter Price G Check out page 52.**

My Fair Lady, Theatre Royal, Drury Lane, describes what is common in many societies: that accent determines social standing and economic opportunity. This famous musical also provides an introduction to the study of phonetics. Theatre tours can be arranged, workshops and educational material is available for school visits, 0207 439 3062. Schools **Winter Price on application.**

The Phantom of the Opera, Her Majesty's Theatre, is a magical story evoking ideas and concepts that run through history and literature: the changing mythology of beauty and the beast, the use of the mask and the power of music. Backstage tours can be arranged and educational material is available, 020 7439 3062. Schools **Winter Price on application.**

of

If you have any helpful suggestions of places we have overlooked which may be suitable for inclusion in this guide or if you have any ideas of ways to improve this guide for the future we shall be pleased to hear from you. Thank you.

Suggestion/Comment _____

_____

_____

_____

_____

_____

_____

_____

_____

_____

_____

_____

Name: _____

Address: _____

_____

_____

Postcode _____

Email address _____

Tick box if you would like to be on our Mailing List _____ ☐

Please return to: Cube Publications, 290 Lymington Road, Highcliffe, Dorset BH23 5ET.

Index